Land Drains
Fences.
Boundary Fences
Water, Pipes Etc.
Underground Wires
Sewers Etc.

Approximate Map
of
Hill Stead Farm

Buildings
Woods
Roads
Swampy

HILL-STEAD

Hill-Stead

THE COUNTRY PLACE OF
Theodate Pope Riddle

JAMES F. O'GORMAN, EDITOR

ESSAYS BY
Edward S. Cooke, Jr.
Allyson M. Hayward
Anne Higonnet
James F. O'Gorman
Robert M. Thorson

FOREWORD BY
Robert A. M. Stern

PRINCETON ARCHITECTURAL PRESS, NEW YORK

Published by
Princeton Architectural Press
37 East Seventh Street
New York, New York 10003

For a free catalog of books, call 1.800.722.6657.
Visit our website at www.papress.com.

Acquisitions Editor: Nancy Eklund Later
Project Editor: Carolyn Deuschle
Designer: Deb Wood

Special thanks to: Nettie Aljian, Bree Anne Apperley,
Sara Bader, Nicola Bednarek, Janet Behning, Becca
Casbon, Carina Cha, Tom Cho, Penny (Yuen Pik)
Chu, Russell Fernandez, Pete Fitzpatrick, Wendy
Fuller, Jan Haux, Linda Lee, Laurie Manfra, John
Myers, Katharine Myers, Steve Royal, Dan Simon,
Andrew Stepanian, Jennifer Thompson, Paul Wagner,
and Joseph Weston of Princeton Architectural Press
—Kevin C. Lippert, publisher

Library of Congress Cataloging-in-Publication Data

Hill-stead : the country place of theodate pope riddle
/ James F. O'Gorman, editor ; essays by Edward
S. Cooke, Jr. ... [et al.] ; contributions by Melanie
Anderson Bourbeau and Cynthia A. Cormier ;
foreword by Robert A.M. Stern.—1st ed.
    p. cm.
Includes bibliographical references and index.
ISBN 978-1-56898-759-0
1. Hill-Stead Museum. 2. Riddle, Theodate Pope,
1867–1946—Homes and haunts—Connecticut—
Farmington. 3. Country homes—Connecticut—
Farmington. 4. Colonial revival (Architecture)—
Connecticut—Farmington. 5. Farmington
(Conn.)—Buildings, structures, etc. 6. Riddle,
Theodate Pope, 1867–1946—Art collections.
7. Art—Private collections—Connecticut—
Farmington. I. O'Gorman, James F. II. Cooke,
Edward S., Jr. III. Bourbeau, Melanie Anderson. IV.
Cormier, Cynthia A.
N569.H55 2010
728.809746'2—dc22
                                2009042466

CONTENTS

HILL-STEAD IS MUCH MORE than a comfortable country house. It is an act of personal reinvention for its principal designer, Theodate Pope (February 2, 1867–August 30, 1946). The headstrong daughter of Alfred Atmore Pope (1842–1913) and Ada Brooks Pope (1844–1920), prosperous and prominent Clevelanders whose origins only two generations before lay in hardscrabble farming in New England, was born Effie. At the age of 19, she renamed herself Theodate, meaning "gift of God," the name of her paternal grandmother from Maine. But a change of name was not enough for the imperious and ambitious Effie: so inspired by the New England landscape and the local culture that she witnessed as a student at Miss Porter's School in Farmington, Connecticut, she began drawing plans for the homestead of her dreams. After the customary Grand Tour of Europe with her parents, she was presented to high society back in Cleveland. That was a disaster, and as soon as she was able, Theodate engineered her escape back to Farmington, buying and restoring a colonial farmhouse on forty-two acres of land that began to fulfill one of her adolescent "air castles" of living on a farm.

But the ambitious Theodate found that the renovation had not satiated her need to create. She decided that the only way to sufficiently utilize her artistic talents and express her idealistic nature was to become a professional architect, despite the fact that the profession of architecture at the time (shortly before the turn of the twentieth century) was virtually closed to women. She instead enlisted the aid of private tutors.

Hill-Stead's Mount Vernon–inspired portico and west front as seen from the entry drive

What then transpired is truly amazing. Theodate persuaded her parents to move East, not to New York City, as many rich Midwesterners such as the Fricks, Carnegies, Phippses, and the Rockefellers were doing, but to rural Farmington. It was a brilliant strategy to launch her professional career while realizing her private cultural agenda. With the promise of a commission for a big house to incorporate her parents' art collection—Impressionist paintings purchased by the Popes in Europe—Theodate, then entering her thirties, was able to entice the renowned architectural firm of McKim, Mead & White to produce professional drawings of her ideas for a country house.

Looking back, it is amazing how similar in temperament Theodate was to another imperious self-inventor—the architect Frank Lloyd Wright (1867–1959), with whom she shared a birth year. Wright also hated the Midwest and was able to escape it—in his case, by jettisoning a wife and six children and fleeing to Italy with a lover. More importantly, he too was intent on creating the quintessential American house. Like Wright, Theodate rejected the European palace model popular in the late nineteenth century, which for her reeked of the new money and pretensions she had detested since childhood. Whereas Wright's commanding talent propelled him toward abstraction and innovation, Theodate's more modest gifts led her toward an architecture of representation and narration. Wright remained provincial—a man of the prairie, which he loathed but could not escape. Theodate was cosmopolitan, but she longed to be provincial—to be rooted in her beloved corner of Connecticut. While Wright mythologized the prairie but did so on his own artistic terms, Theodate embraced the New England vernacular, not in an effort to reinvent it but to explore its nuances.

Theodate believed deeply that historical allusion could give meaning to the present. In rewriting her past she cast her parents in the role of New England gentry, just as she had once reformulated herself from Effie to Theodate. The design for Hill-Stead did not slavishly copy its model, Mount Vernon, the Virginia home of George Washington designed in 1743 by its principal resident. Repeating only the essential feature, its two-story porch, Theodate based the rest of the design on an idealized version of the New England farmhouse and sited it on a 250-acre working farm.

At first glance the house may seem like just another in a long series of houses modeled after the first president's. These include the James Breese house of 1898, in Southampton, New York, by McKim, Mead & White (which, significantly, began as a farmhouse) as well as the Robert J. Collier house of 1914, by John Russell Pope (no relation). The Mount Vernon model reached some sort of apotheosis in the 1930s, in the Wickatunk, New Jersey, home and office of David O. Selznick, producer of the

film *Gone with the Wind* (1939), and in the subsequent decade, in the various Howard Johnson restaurants built throughout New England. But closer inspection reveals Hill-Stead's lively syncopation of facade elements, especially the colonnade played off against an antiphonal arrangement of bay windows. Inside, the Georgian regularity of Washington's house is abandoned in favor of a sophisticated spatial arrangement relating to McKim, Mead & White's Shingle Style work of the 1880s, with bold crisscrossing diagonal vistas leading the eye to carefully placed paintings. Hill-Stead, to a remarkable degree, is both monumental and informal—no trivial accomplishment. It is a mansion and a farmhouse. Most of all, it is quintessentially an American house.

Theodate carried on at Hill-Stead long after her parents finished out their years there, maintaining the house and its collections, overseeing the daily workings of the farm, and running her architectural practice out of a studio she fashioned from an existing nineteenth-century house on the property. But throughout this time, the architectural accomplishments at Hill-Stead largely escaped recognition. Even Philip Johnson (1906–2005), one of America's most important architects of the post–World War II era, failed to see its value for a very long time. Johnson, another self-inventing Clevelander, was an occasional visitor to his "Aunt Effie's" house (Johnson's mother, Louise, was Theodate's first cousin). A passionate modernist singularly committed

View from Entry Hall into the home's expansive and art-filled Drawing Room

to the International Style in the 1920s and 1930s, Johnson told me that by the
1950s the house was not even considered to be a work of architecture. Moreover,
its Impressionist art was belittled as just "a collection of bad pictures." "It was very
unfashionable" Johnson explained, "to like the collection of art at Hill-Stead. *Haystacks*,
by then, had become postcards." Today, with our more inclusive, postmodern mindset,
Hill-Stead is once again to be appreciated, both as a collection of important works
of art and as architecture—indeed, as among the most representative examples of
American architecture of its time.

Alfred, Ada, and
Theodate Pope at
Hill-Stead, ca. 1902

IN 1947, ITS FIRST YEAR of operation, Hill-Stead Museum hosted just under 3,000 patrons. Most, undoubtedly, were drawn to the former country estate of Alfred Atmore Pope (1842–1913) and Ada Brooks Pope (1844–1920) by its world-class Impressionist art collection, which was displayed in situ, just as it had been during the lifetime of their daughter, Theodate Pope (1867–1946), the estate's inheritor, protector, and architect. Indeed, Theodate's last will and testament provided that the main house remain "the same forever as a Museum for the exhibition of the articles of artistic interest"—a provision that has been respected and largely upheld to the present day.

Tucked away in a bucolic Connecticut town, somewhat off the beaten path that connects the cultural centers of Boston and New York, Hill-Stead has always been recognized as a jewel by the art enthusiasts and scholars who have found their way to its door. But although the initial focus of the museum may have been on its art, there is much more about Hill-Stead that warrants our attention. During the past few decades in particular, the focus of art history has expanded to include the history of art patronage, collecting patterns, and even framing and display techniques. In addition to the fine arts, architecture, landscape design, and the decorative arts have become subjects of increased interest. Local and national history has grown in popularity, with the Colonial Revival period (during which Hill-Stead was built) garnering particular attention. Add to these advances a growing interest in historic preservation and women's studies, and it is clear that the climate for appreciating Hill-Stead is vastly different from previous eras when, as one long-time staff member recalls, "everything we knew [about the house and its collections] fit on one index card per room."

Today our context for understanding Hill-Stead, its architecture, interior design and furnishings, art and decorative

View from the North Porch, over the pond toward the farm complex

art, gardens, farm, and landscape extends across disciplines. In addition, research directly related to Theodate's pioneering career as an architect and to her parents' avant-garde collecting habits has added remarkable texture and detail to the general historical outline. Hill-Stead's architecture has been the subject of numerous investigations including, most recently, a Historic American Buildings Survey (HABS), carried out by the National Park Service. Its architectural significance has earned it designation as a National Historic Landmark and an official project of Save America's Treasures. Research on Hill-Stead's rich natural setting conducted under the auspices of a state-funded Historic Landscape Report has unearthed deep connections in the horticultural, geological, agricultural, and garden design history of the property, further enhancing its story.

Having accomplished all of this research, the time is ripe to share the story of Theodate and Hill-Stead with a larger audience. This publication collects from all of the current research and disciplinary trends to examine Hill-Stead from multiple angles, from the use of architectural precedents in its design to the strategic placement of pictures as the focal point of rooms, to the construction of outdoor living spaces enclosed by vernacular stone walls. It clarifies some attribution issues that have been raised over the design of the house and its gardens and gives Theodate, at last, the full credit she deserves. In short, it presents a new and engaging portrait of Hill-Stead and its creator that broadens the definition of "articles of artistic interest" to include far more than just world-class Impressionist paintings.

Although numerous articles, essays, and guidebooks have appeared over the years, written by museum staff members, volunteers, consultants, and researchers, this book stands alone as the definitive piece of scholarship regarding Theodate Pope Riddle and Hill-Stead. We owe a great debt of gratitude to the accomplished authors— all leaders in their field—who contributed notes and essays to this book: James F. O'Gorman, Robert A. M. Stern, Edward S. Cooke, Jr., Anne Higonnet, Allyson M. Hayward, and Robert M. Thorson. The new scholarship (and friendships) that have resulted from their research, conducted over many years and many visits to the museum and its archives, provide the substance of this volume. It has been our distinct pleasure to work with all.

We acknowledge Hill-Stead Museum's former director, Linda Steigleder, for her commitment to this project and wish to thank all of our colleagues at Hill-Stead, past and present, who offered insights and encouragement throughout the preparation of this book, especially archivist Polly Huntington. The project would not have been possible without the generous support of the State of Connecticut, Special Act Grant; the Jane Henson Foundation; *Furthermore*, a program of the J. M. Kaplan Fund; the Edward C. and Ann T. Roberts Foundation; the Ann and Erlo van Waveren Foundation; Mott Corporation; the late Bertha Brooks McCormick; and many other generous and valued supporters. Others who deserve special thanks include the editorial and design staff at Princeton Architectural Press, particularly Nancy Eklund Later and Deb Wood, and the photographers whose work enriches this volume: James Rosenthal, Patty Swanson, Jerry L. Thompson, and Lesley Unruh.

Since its opening in 1947, more than 700,000 patrons have experienced Hill-Stead, through guided tours, school programs, lectures, nature walks, family festivities, and, of course, the acclaimed Sunken Garden Poetry and Music Festival. Our hope is that this book will enhance the appreciation of this wonderful place for those who visit and enrich the experience of the next generation of museum visitors and patrons.

—*Melanie Anderson Bourbeau* AND *Cynthia A. Cormier*

"A GREAT NEW HOUSE on a hilltop that overlooked the most composed of communities," the novelist Henry James declared, an "exquisite palace of peace, and light and harmony."[1] "A large, rambling, old fashioned looking house with wide verandahs and big, comfortable, low-ceiled rooms," wrote artist Kenyon Cox, "the general effect is of coolness and freshness and light, the paintings harmonizing admirably with the airy brightness of such a country house."[2] "Hill-Stead fits its place and purpose in a way that sets it apart from other grand estates containing art collections," wrote the historian Mark Hewitt, "…making it perhaps the finest Colonial revival house in the United States."[3]

Hill-Stead has always attracted the attention of historians, writers, artists, and architects. Publications about their new house, its furnishings, and its setting overlooking the village of Farmington, Connecticut, began to appear in the national press soon after Alfred Atmore Pope (1842–1913) and Ada Brooks Pope (1844–1920) moved into their country estate in 1901. *The Architectural Review* for November 1902 and *The Architectural Record* for August 1906 featured photographs of the exterior, interiors, and original formal garden in multiple pages. Captions pointed to the harmony of the furnishings and architecture, and commented on the "attractive," "tasteful," "interesting," and "inviting" nature of the place. The first substantive discussion of Hill-Stead appeared in *American Homes and Gardens* in February 1910.

Hill-Stead's main house, barn, and carriage house in center (framed by the Sunken Garden in foreground and pond in background)

It was written by the distinguished historian, connoisseur, and critic Barr Ferree, who described the house, its furnishings, and its landscape setting in some detail. He recognized the rural New England roots and domestic character of the structure's elongated layout and noted with approval its openness of plan. He emphasized the appropriateness of a house that revived

Colonial and Federal forms in an old New England town. It was not a reproduction, he assured his readers, "but a quiet harmonious design, worked out in the style of the period, with detailing of the most careful kind, a house that is at once scholarly and refined, modern and old."[4]

Ferree assigned the design of the house to the New York architectural office of McKim, Mead & White, as had previous publications and as would later ones, "supplemented with the zealous assistance" of the Popes' daughter, Theodate, "to whom much of the interior treatment is due."[5] This separation of male architect and female decorator is to be expected in an era when a female architect scarcely existed. In some other discussions, both contemporary and more recent, we read similar equivocal statements, such as that Theodate is usually given much of the credit for the house designed by McKim, Mead & White, or that it was a unique collaboration between Theodate and McKim, Mead & White. As we shall see, however, the project is more accurately described as designed by Theodate Pope with the support of the McKim office.

The first publications about Hill-Stead appeared in the early twentieth century, at the height of popularity of the cultural ideals that so well exemplified the place. In architecture, these ideals underpinned a movement usually called the Colonial Revival but more accurately styled the English Colonial and/or Federal Revival; in the decorative arts, the Arts and Crafts movement (in its New England manifestation); in painting, the current vogue among some American collectors for French Impressionism; in landscape, the English Picturesque tradition, wed to the expectations of the owners of a turn-of-the-twentieth-century country estate. As the influence of these movements waned with the arrival of modernism, Hill-Stead's reputation dimmed for a time, and it came to be seen as representative of a low point in American cultural history. As Robert A. M. Stern points out in his foreword, the distinguished and committed modern architect Philip Johnson—a cousin of Theodate Pope—failed to appreciate the architecture or its contents.

With the dawn of postmodernism, the inevitable cycle of taste returned interest in the Colonial Revival and its associated movements, along with all other historical modes of past design. Serious and appreciative discussions about Hill-Stead began to reappear in books and periodicals. Well-rounded articles on its history popped up in magazines such as Country Life (1987) and Antiques (1988), and more recently, in books such as Richard Guy Wilson's The Colonial Revival House (2004) and Roderic H. Blackburn and Geoffrey Gross' Great Houses of New England (2008). These recent discussions make it clear that Hill-Stead is now seen as a canonical image of turn-of-the-twentieth-century American culture.

Justly celebrated, Hill-Stead is now a much-visited destination, open year-round to the public. It began, however, as a private family retreat. At the death of her parents, Theodate inherited the estate, and at her death in 1946 she left the house as a museum "of articles of artistic interest."[6] It then became a house museum, a type of cultural institution that came into existence as early as 1837 in London, with the opening of Sir John Soane's Museum. There, as at Hill-Stead, a house of the architect's design served as the setting for the display of his collection of furnishings, art, and artifacts. In New England, contemporary examples included the Isabella Stewart Gardner Museum in Boston (1903) and Beauport, the Henry Davis Sleeper House in Gloucester, Massachusetts (begun 1907), open to the public in 1903 and 1942, respectively. In these institutions, the residence was built around patterns of living and entertaining but with an eye to the future public display of decorative and fine arts in a domestic atmosphere. As Anne Higonnet points out in her essay, many of these institutions were formed by independent-minded women such as Theodate Pope.

The present publication is part of the revival of Hill-Stead's reputation. As public interest and visitation increase, it seemed desirable to take a fresh and comprehensive look at Hill-Stead *tout entière*. Five historians have produced four essays and a note on five different aspects of the Hill-Stead experience. They have restudied the existing site and reexamined published and unpublished documents both verbal and visual, such as letters, diaries, drawings, photographs, and paintings, in order to assess Hill-Stead in its historical context. The institution's archives are especially rich in such material. Although the authors' specific subjects and their methods of approach differ, what emerges from this reexamination of Hill-Stead is an exposition on the site that is as integrated as the place itself.

As we have seen, the Hill-Stead experience as a whole is composed of architecture, decorative arts, art, and landscape design. It stands at the crossroads of currents in each of these fields around 1900. I point in my essay to two important issues raised by the architecture of the house: its inspiration by American stylistic tradition as it was understood at the time, and the historically misunderstood identity of the designer.

In the wake of the United States Centennial Celebration of 1876, the nation rediscovered its past—especially its English Colonial and early Federal past. Books and buildings steeped in Colonial and Federal forms began to appear in profusion. Patrons and architects intended to infuse a sense of national history and of regional tradition into new buildings through the study and use of past styles. By 1900, other houses like Hill-Stead, derived from traditional New England plans (some even similarly embellished with a Mount Vernon–style portico) and furnished with period pieces, were being designed to proclaim themselves American places, and their inhabitants as deeply rooted American citizens. Within this group, Hill-Stead was exceptional in its choice collection of Impressionist paintings, the relative quality of its design, and in the gender of its chief architect.

When the Pope family decided to build a home in Farmington, it sought the aid of one of the foremost architectural firms working in the English Colonial/ Federal Revival style, a firm among the most celebrated in the history of American architecture—McKim, Mead & White of New York. This has long led to a misunderstanding about the true designer of the house. Female architects were almost unknown at the time, and Theodate then had no credentials as a designer. Critics—male critics—long scoffed at the idea of "Miss Pope" as architect of the house, but the records—letters, notes, drawings—and Theodate's method of working on the house compared to that of her male contemporaries clearly show that she did indeed conceive the plan and supervise the construction of a design merely drafted by the firm. Judging by her own experience with Colonial architecture in her earlier house in Farmington, and by some of the books preserved in her library, such as Joy Wheeler Dow's *American Renaissance*, she thoroughly intended to create the look of a "traditional American" house.

The English Colonial/Federal style carries into the house as the primary historical reference. Since the arrangement of the interior has not remained static, to describe the original furnishings and their historical context Edward S. Cooke, Jr., relied on identifying remaining pieces as seen in vintage photographs and a 1909 inventory. The Popes' previous house in Cleveland, a Romanesque Revival structure designed by well-known Boston architect William Ralph Emerson, had been furnished in a way that leaned toward the English Arts and Crafts movement, led by the celebrated designer William Morris. This was a movement that prized preindustrial, often medieval, sources in the production of crafted or craft look-alike furnishings. The Arts and Crafts movement in America is generally seen as progressive and proto-modern, and in the hands of a Gustav Stickley or a Frank Lloyd Wright, it was that. In New

England, however, preindustrial meant Colonial or early republican forms, and many of the products of the movement were indistinguishable from the English Colonial/Federal revival.[7] Where Wright sought change, New England sought continuity.

The area's answer to Wright was Wallace Nutting, an equally renowned designer of reproduction Colonial furniture. At Hill-Stead the Popes (for as Cooke makes clear, all three members of the family were engaged in creating a suitable interior for their country estate) sought a combination of old furniture and decorative objects and pieces that stemmed from producers and shops that specialized in reproduction designs. Cooke's analysis of the result of arranging these various parts emphasizes the coherent pattern achieved in each of the principal rooms. The furnishings in general displayed an eclectic mix, writes Cooke, that fits the prescriptions of contemporary writers on the subject, but finds its only real parallel in "color, material, and form" at this period at Henry Sleeper's Beauport.

Both Cooke and Higonnet discuss the prints displayed at Hill-Stead. Those hung along the main stair reflect the renewed interest in printmaking known as the

Hill-Stead southwest elevation. *The Architectural Record*, August 1906.

The Popes' Romanesque Revival townhouse in the city of Cleveland, Ohio, was designed for them between 1883–1885. This earlier home was far different from the country place they built for themselves in Farmington, Connecticut, less than twenty years later.

Print Revival, which began in this country in the 1870s and 1880s. The Japanese prints also collected by Alfred Pope paralleled his painting collection, for the Impressionists were avid students of the colored woodblock made available after the opening of Japan to the West at midcentury. Cooke also emphasizes the central role of the paintings in the décor. He notes that Theodate's interior architecture and the family's furnishings are closely integrated in form and color with the paintings, that they are designed to make the paintings the main features of important rooms and enjoyed as such.

Higonnet and Cooke also agree on the relationship between the painting collection and its domestic setting. Higonnet finds Hill-Stead special because it displays Impressionist works as they were intended to be seen. In such an intimate setting, they could be viewed comfortably and seen individually, in contrast to the way they have come to be seen, in crowded exhibitions in large public museums. The collection was the passion of Alfred Pope, but daughter Theodate had her impact, for in Higonnet's thinking, she had a "collection museum" in mind from early on. Alfred Pope bought wisely and well. As a businessman himself, he found congenial the businesslike approach of the Impressionists, especially Monet, according to Higonnet.

He bought boldly, trusting his eye, seeking out real quality. It might be supposed that a man of his time and station would have looked for more conservative works, but these he rejected in favor of cutting-edge, modern art, although he seems to have chosen traditional subjects rather than the urban or industrial scenes that marked much Impressionist production.

Hill-Stead, with its Colonial trimmings and Mount Vernon–style portico, period furnishings and Impressionist paintings, stands in the midst of a rolling landscape shaped by geology and art. Allyson M. Hayward discusses the natural and artificial molding of the site and puts it into the context of the English picturesque landscape tradition, which began in the eighteenth century, and more contemporary trends such as the country place movement, which saw the erection of large estates where experimental farming was carried out, as at Hill-Stead, under the watchful eyes of the owners. The large site was assembled from a number of parcels purchased when the project began, individual units that were drawn into a whole controlled by Theodate with some still-not-clearly-understood initial help from the landscape architect Warren Manning. They selected and shaped the location of the house, shifted large trees into place near it, created an artificial pond, laid out a six-hole "golf grounds," dairy farm, and orchard, and, most importantly, skillfully composed stone walls laced through the site, as Robert Thorson's note so well evokes.

Not all of this has survived the passage of time. A formal "Sunken Garden" that originally stood to the south of the house, the special project of Ada Pope and perhaps designed by Theodate, can only be understood from vintage photographs. As Hayward says, it and its summer house extended the Colonial aura of the place and thus fit the general conception of the whole enterprise. A subsequent plan for the site designed by friend and famed landscape architect Beatrix Farrand has been meticulously reclaimed after careful study of the planting plan, and after extensive research into Farrand's sense of design and preferred plants, numerous visits to other Farrand gardens, and examination of her other planting plans. Hayward links the adjacent Walking, or Wild, Garden to books by the Irishman William Robinson. The integration of English and Colonial/Federal characteristics we find in the house extends into its surroundings as well.

The essays included in this volume are enriched by a profusion of primary documents, drawings, and archival photographs, which illuminate the domestic site designed by Theodate Pope for her parents and, just as importantly, the lives lived within it. New color photography beautifully conveys the qualities of house and landscape as they exist today. In words and pictures this book artfully reveals the history and ongoing vitality of, as Stern describes it, one of "the most representative examples of the American architecture of one hundred years ago."

As is so often the case in the careers of architects, Theodate Pope's first "commission" stemmed from her family. After Hill-Stead she gradually became registered as a professional architect in Connecticut and New York State, and the Englishness of her work intensified as she traveled to the Cotswolds and elsewhere in Britain in search of inspiration. In her later private houses and educational complexes, she followed the lead of British Arts and Crafts designers to produce a few of the most impressive architectural designs in this country in the early years of the twentieth century. A wealthy woman, she remained a nonconformist in a profession still largely ruled by men, and it has been only in recent years that her work has begun to receive the close attention—and appreciation—that is its due. The present publication celebrates the beginning of her extraordinary career.

Grainstacks, White Frost Effect, Claude Monet (1889), hangs over a sofa in a corner of the Drawing Room.

SEPTEMBER 14 1900 (AGE 33)

FOR YEARS I HAVE BEEN KEEN ON ARCHITECTURE AND FELT THAT THE UGLINESS OF OUR BUILDINGS ACTUALLY MENACED MY HAPPINESS AND FELT BREATHLESSLY THAT I MUST HELP IN THE CAUSE OF GOOD ARCHITECTURE.

MY INTEREST IN ARCHITECTURE HAS ALWAYS BEEN MORE INTENSE THAN MY INTEREST IN ANY OTHER ART MANIFESTATION, AND ON MY WORD I THINK IT IS NOT DEAD YET——NOT QUITE. IF I ONLY KNEW HOW TO HELP THE CAUSE OF GOOD ARCHITECTURE! BUT I AM TIRED OF SEEING THESE FLUTED FLIMSY HIGHLY COLORED HEN HOUSES GOING UP——AND AM TIRED GNASHING MY TEETH OVER THEM.

Theodate Pope,
Hill-Stead architect,
1915

A BIOGRAPHICAL SKETCH OF THE POPE FAMILY
Melanie Anderson Bourbeau and Cynthia A. Cormier

THE POPES WERE A FAMILY of three—parents who came from modest means and worked their way up in society, and a child of privilege who continually looked back to her family's New England farming roots. To fully appreciate Hill-Stead—the Popes' country home and Theodate Pope's first architectural project—a brief introduction to each family member is useful.

Alfred Atmore Pope (1842–1913) epitomized the self-made man of the nineteenth century. In 1866 he took advantage of opportunities that placed him in the "right place at the right time." He married his childhood sweetheart, Ada Brooks (1844–1920), and for the first few years of their marriage continued to work alongside his father and brothers in his family's woolen business. His career began its ascent when he made the decision to strike out in a new direction. Born in Maine, he moved with his family to Ohio when they relocated their textile business in the years before the Civil War. In 1869, after borrowing heavily from his wife's family, Pope bought into the newly formed Cleveland Malleable Iron Company and secured a position as secretary and treasurer. Ten years after joining the company, at the age of thirty-seven, he rose to the rank of president.

During the formative years of their company's growth, Pope and his associates were guided by the experience of J. H. Whittemore, who ran a successful malleable iron concern in Naugatuck, Connecticut. With Whittemore's backing and support, the Cleveland firm prospered and eventually incorporated several malleable iron operations throughout the Midwest, which were consolidated into the National Malleable Castings Company in 1891. An exceptionally strong form of the

Alfred Pope's many business activities provided him with the resources needed to build two grand homes for his family, collect fine art, and travel abroad. Pope is seated in the center, with his associates, ca. 1890.

Alfred Pope seated on the North Porch, smoking a cigar, and sporting his golfing attire

metal—much stronger than forged iron—malleable iron could withstand extreme shock and thus was of great use in the burgeoning railroad industry. Through foresight, productivity, and sound investment Alfred Pope became a wealthy man. As he moved up the social ladder, he surrounded himself and his family with all the trappings suitable to their station. Hiring a prominent Boston architect, Pope had an impressive house in the fashionable Romanesque Revival style built on Euclid Avenue, in one of Cleveland's most tony districts. Among his neighbors was the wealthy industrialist and philanthropist John D. Rockefeller.

After thirty-two years working in the malleable iron industry in Cleveland, Pope was ready for a change of scenery. At the urging of his daughter (and only child), Theodate (1867–1946), he and his wife moved to Farmington, Connecticut, and took up residence at Hill-Stead in June 1901. The home's name was chosen, quite simply, because it was a homestead perched at the top of a hill. Pope had long harbored an interest in farming, to the extent that he wanted to be able to provide his family with fresh eggs, butter, and milk; here, amidst the backdrop of the Litchfield Hills, he and his daughter could finally play at being farmers. Pope remained active in business during his years in Farmington, but allowed himself to take time out of his daily activities to indulge in favorite pastimes. He attended an occasional baseball game and played golf on his personal six-hole golf grounds, conveniently located on the 250-acre property, just outside the door of his office.

Another favorite pastime of Pope's—one he approached with great passion and discernment—was collecting art. His penchant for Impressionist paintings, with their boldness and immediacy, placed him within a select group of American connoisseurs at the turn of the twentieth century, and distinguished him from many of his peers, whose traditional tastes gravitated only toward Old Master paintings and drawings. Favoring quality over quantity, Pope took home only the best of what he saw, including what are now considered seminal works by Mary Cassatt (1844–1926), Edgar Degas (1834–1917), Edouard Manet (1832–1883), Claude Monet (1840–1926), and James Abbott McNeill Whistler (1834–1903).

Pope did not limit his collecting to Impressionism alone. He also acquired paintings by mainstream artists of the period including Pierre Puvis de Chavannes (1824–1898) and Eugène Carrière (1849–1906), as well as Asian, American, and European prints—etchings, mezzotints, and woodblocks. In addition, he surrounded himself with decorative art objects, including bronze sculpture and Asian and European porcelains.

Ada Brooks Pope on
third-floor deck atop
front portico, ca. 1902

In Farmington, Theodate lived a simple life in her eigtheenth-century saltbox she named the O'Rourkery. While working on the renovations to this house, Theodate decided to become an architect. In this photograph, Theodate and her best friend and teacher, Mary Hillard, peel apples on the porch.

Theodate Pope shown (right) with her cousin Elizabeth "Betty" Brooks (left). Both girls came to Farmington to attend Miss Porter's School in 1886.

Theodate Pope and classmates
from Miss Porter's School, ca. 1887.
Theodate (center), her favorite
cousin, Elizabeth (Betty) Brooks
(far right), cousins Alice and Agnes
Hamilton, back row.

FEBRUARY 12 1886 (AGE 19)

I WONDER WHY MY MIND OCCUPIES ITSELF WITH NOTHING SAVE THOUGHTS OF THE COUNTRY, NOWADAYS. I NEVER LONGED SO TO BE IN THE WOODS, UNDER THE GREEN LEAVES. THOUGHTS OF THE VERMONT WOODS ARE WITH ME MOST OF THE TIME. WILL I EVER LIVE IN THE COUNTRY, HAVE A COUNTRY HOUSE, NEAR THE WOODS? I THINK THEY WOULD REALLY INSPIRE ME, I MIGHT PERHAPS WRITE QUITE PRETTY FAIRY TALES IF I WERE ONLY NEAR THE ABODES OF FAIRIES AND ELVES.

JULY 2, 1886 (AGE 19)

I SHALL WRITE MISS WINTERS [*her beloved teacher*] OF MY FAVORITE AIR CASTLE, THAT OF OWNING A FINE COUNTRY HOME IN THE EAST, A DAIRY FARM, HAVE HER LIVE WITH ME AND THEN BRING CHILDREN WHO ARE POOR TO SPEND THE SUMMER AND PERHAPS WHOLE YEAR WITH US. WE CAN WORK FOR THEIR BENEFIT IN MANY WAYS, WHILE I CAN ALWAYS HAVE A MODEL TO DRAW.

WEDNESDAY MAY 21, 1890 (AGE 23)

IT IS <u>DECIDED. I AM TO HAVE A LITTLE HOUSE IN FARMINGTON</u>! MAMA AND PAPA THINK I HAVE BEEN LONGING FOR THE COUNTRY THAT NOW I CAN HAVE IT. AND THEY ALSO THINK IT WILL BE GOOD FOR MY HEALTH TO HAVE THE QUIET OUT-OF-DOOR LIFE I WOULD HAVE THERE. FARMINGTON IS OF COURSE THE PLACE FOR ME TO GO AS I HAVE SO MANY FRIENDS THERE. I AM TO SEE ABOUT RENTING A COTTAGE WHEN I AM THERE ON THIS TRIP THEN I AM TO SEE TO THE FURNISHING OF IT MYSELF, BEARING IN MIND OF COURSE THAT TOO MUCH MONEY MUST NOT BE SPENT ON IT. I AM TO HAVE A GUERNSEY COW, A PIG & CHICKENS, ALSO A GARDEN & PERHAPS BEES.

If Alfred Pope's life exemplified the strivings and ideals of the Gilded Age, his daughter Theodate's was both a product of and a reaction to the same. Born and raised in Ohio, Theodate first attended a private girls' school, alongside the daughters of presidents James Garfield and Rutherford B. Hayes. At age nineteen, she was sent East to continue her education at Miss Porter's School in the village of Farmington, Connecticut, between 1886 and 1888. There, she fell in love with a romanticized version of rural life in America.

After finishing her course work at Miss Porter's, Theodate spent nearly a year traveling with her parents to over forty cities throughout Europe. She joined her father on trips to museums, art dealers' galleries, and private collections, and learned first hand about the Impressionists. While on the Grand Tour, she decided against marrying her first suitor, Harris Whittemore (the son of Pope's mentor and business partner), and discussed possible career paths with her father. She sketched and made notes on buildings and scenes, especially while visiting the English countryside. She dreamed of a simple life of owning and operating a small farm. Gradually, Theodate's plans to design and build an English Colonial-style farmstead coalesced, encouraged by her father's own desire to own a country estate back East near friends and family.

Upon the family's return from Europe, Theodate made her debut into Cleveland society at the age of twenty-one. Finding the lifestyle of a debutante superficial and unrewarding, she prevailed upon her parents to let her return to Farmington, where she felt infinitely more at home. This time, she would begin life on her own, and live it on her own terms. A child of privilege, she refused her destiny as a society matron in order to pursue a career in architecture. Theodate's parents acquiesced, her father's personal and financial support providing her with a safety net, should she falter.

Theodate rented an "old brown house" not far from Miss Porter's School: an eighteenth-century saltbox that she named "The O'Rourkery" and eventually bought. Directing the restoration of the house initiated her practical training as an architect. Rather than attending one of the few architecture schools open to women or apprenticing with an established firm (then an unlikely option for a woman of her class), she would learn on the job. In the restored house she realized her dream: living simply, if by her own well-heeled standards.

Theodate was not unique in her restoration endeavor. In 1890 the English Colonial Revival was at its height, and throughout New England upper-class women were saving old houses and restoring them according to a romanticized vision of

RIGHT: At the age of 49, Theodate Pope married diplomat and linguist John Wallace Riddle. Photograph taken on their wedding day, May 6, 1916.

BELOW: After taking up residency in their new home in Farmington, Alfred and Ada Pope spent quite a bit of time entertaining family and friends. Posed under the portico, Alfred stands in the center, with Ada seated below, surrounded by a small group of Brooks family members. The family pets also joined the photo.

how people had lived in the colonial era. During the 1880s and 1890s, Farmington's own Village Improvement Society worked to "clean up" the town and emphasize its colonial heritage. Accurate historic preservation based on sound research arrived several decades later. Theodate, for instance, changed the exterior of the O'Rourkery from brown to a light color, probably white, even though white paint was rarely, if ever, available in colonial times.

Throughout Alfred's career and Theodate's schooling, Ada tended to her family and their home. Ada Brooks was born in Salem, Ohio, the third of eight children. By 1862, when she was eighteen, both of her parents had died. Perhaps for this reason, Ada and her siblings remained very close to each other throughout their lives, often gathering in Vermont where their parents had been born. Following her marriage to Alfred, Ada made directing the Pope household her life's work, as was the custom of nineteenth-century American women of privilege; she accomplished this task with legendary skill and grace. While at first less than enthusiastic about the move to Farmington, she adapted to country living. It was she who acquired many of the furnishings at Hill-Stead and created its stylish yet comfortable environment.

Ada never fully recovered from her husband's death in 1913. In her later years, she found it difficult to spend long, lonely winters at Hill-Stead and rather, spent increasing amounts of time in California with her Brooks family relatives. Hill-Stead then became home to Theodate and her husband, diplomat John Wallace Riddle, whom she married in 1916.

From 1901 until 1946, the homestead on a hill that had its origins in Theodate's adolescent musings—of living on a farm, raising orphaned children, and starting a school—served as the family's home: first, to Alfred and Ada; then, to Theodate and John and the foster sons they raised there, and also to their seemingly unending stream of houseguests. These included the writers Henry James, Edith Wharton, Sinclair Lewis, Thornton Wilder, and Ida Tarbell; the artist Mary Cassatt; and President Theodore Roosevelt and first lady Eleanor Roosevelt. Today, Hill-Stead continues to welcome guests from near and far and all those who visit leave with an appreciation for this charmed country place created in part by each of the original occupants—Alfred Atmore Pope, Ada Brooks Pope, and Theodate Pope Riddle.

FEBRUARY 3, 1901 (AGE 34)

THIS EVENING MOTHER CAME DOWN TO MY ROOM
& WE PLANNED HOW OUR NOTE PAPER FOR THE
NEW HOME WILL BE STAMPED. WE HAVE DECIDED
TO CALL THE PLACE HILL STEAD——I THOUGHT
OF IT EARLY IN THE BUILDING & MOTHER HAS
ALWAYS LIKED IT WHILE FATHER IS LUKE WARM
BUT SUGGESTS NO OTHER.

It is precisely the kind of house one would naturally look for in Farmington

FARMINGTON, CONNECTICUT, like other affluent New England towns at the turn of the twentieth century, found itself in the throes of nostalgia for its colonial and federal-era past. On a foundation of the 1640s, clapboard houses with gambrel and gabled and saltbox silhouettes rose over the long years beside the river between the hills. This was especially true along Main Street, where, since 1771, the sturdy Congregational Meetinghouse, with its slender spire resting above an airy belfry, has pinned the settlement to its picturesque site.

The town's large collection of pre–Civil War domestic architecture drew special attention, however. In *Farmington, Connecticut: The Village of Beautiful Homes,* a book published in 1906 that unfolded the Anglo-American history and captured the picture-book charm of the place, the writer Julius Gay listed the old houses and named the pioneering families that had erected and occupied them over the years. The inventory celebrated the roots and progress of a self-satisfied America. Gay noted, too, that the town's new architecture reflected a revival of the "Old Colonial style."[1] Indeed, the critic Barr Ferree would write only four year later, "a modern house in Farmington is so much an anomaly as to be quite unthinkable."[2] The most impressive evidence of the Colonial Revival in this prominent New England town is Hill-Stead, the Alfred Atmore Pope house, which was just reaching its definitive form as Gay's tribute appeared.

Hill-Stead stands proudly on a knoll overlooking the village of Farmington, its eponymous river, and surrounding hills. Theodate Pope (1867–1946) designed it as the country retreat of her parents, Alfred Atmore Pope (1842–1913) and Ada Brooks Pope (1844–1920), and it became her home after their deaths. In her will she created the house museum we know today. The

Hill-Stead, west front, as shown in *American Homes and Gardens,* February 1910

family, headed by a successful industrialist, had deep roots in Maine and Vermont, but then lived in Cleveland on posh Euclid Avenue in a house designed by a noted Boston architect. Theodate chose the location for Hill-Stead, on its original 250-acre site, apparently in consultation with landscape architect Warren H. Manning, a protégé of Frederick Law Olmsted, of Central Park fame. She hired the leading New York architectural firm of McKim, Mead & White to draft her design. The house rose between 1898 and 1901, and an extension was built between 1906 and 1907.[3]

The plan of the house is roughly L-shaped, its rambling, disjointed composition accommodating generous, comfortable living spaces. These spaces are expressed in three dimensions by a conglomeration of shapes of various sizes, extended by an arcaded carriage entrance to the south, a temple-front portico to the north, and a colossal portico to the west. The interior of the house is graced by Alfred Pope's choice collection of then cutting-edge paintings and furnished with antique and reproduction "period" furniture. In its forms and details, it is a home that takes its cue from the architectural history of its region, from both the vernacular and high-style traditions of colonial New England and federal-period America. It is a two-and-a-half-story frame house, gable-roofed with prominent dormers, of white-painted clapboards with dark green shutters embracing multipaned sash windows. Private and public rooms occupy the west wing, while the service and servants' rooms (now museum offices) stretch eastward. An attached barn containing carriage shed, stable, carriage house, and, later, Makeshift Theater, are set off from the house visually through the use of clapboards of alternating width, fixed by visible nails with rounded heads.

In addition to being what we now call a trophy house, Hill-Stead was to be a model farm. Its rambling layout was inspired by the traditional New England farmsteads that had been rediscovered and prized since the time of the Centennial Exhibition in 1876. The plan and massing of the house borrow from the "organic" evolution of those old buildings, which accumulated additions over time. The Fairbanks House in Dedham, Massachusetts, begun in 1637/38 and often said to be the oldest surviving frame house in New England, is, with its variety of extensions, the classic surviving example of this vernacular building tradition. The overall layout of Hill-Stead, with living quarters in the west wing and long perpendicular service wing reaching back to the barn, echoes the "continuous" architecture of rural New England.

The high-style interior and exterior details of Hill-Stead, on the other hand, reflect the sophisticated architectural tradition of the Georgian and Federal eras. While 1830 was well beyond the English "colonial" period in what would become the

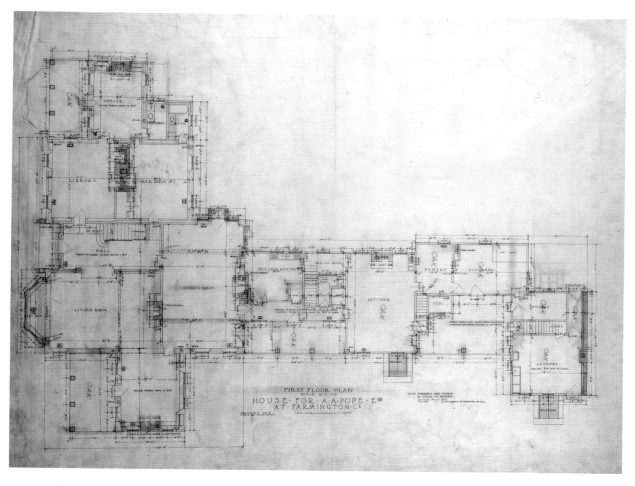

United States, it marked the end of Georgian rule in England and formed a terminus for revivers of the English Colonial and Georgian style. The classical Roman profiles, pediments, and piers of the house's exterior and the three-centered arch and classical fireplace frames of its richly articulated interior speak of a higher societal plane than does its vernacular layout. As is characteristic of the revival house, however, Hill-Stead is an "over elaboration, enlargement, and improvement" on both of its original prototypes.[5] Houses of this kind were not meant to recreate the lifestyle of the past but to draw upon its aura. The Popes enjoyed all the modern conveniences available at the turn of the twentieth century that bespoke a comfortable, upscale, up-to-date domesticity: indoor plumbing, gas (and soon electric) lighting, an elevator, and a central heating and cooling system.[6]

Hill-Stead, First-Floor Plan, McKim, Mead & White Architects, drawing by Egerton Swartwout, 1899

The corner of Hill-Stead's Library houses many of Theodate Pope's books on architecture.

Almost continuously from the 1870s to the present, but especially around 1900, houses inspired by Anglo-American precedents have stood at the center of the American Dream.[7] Why this is so is a question demanding too many answers for this essay. As we shall see, however, there is one important source of the design—and meaning—of Hill-Stead that provides an essential clue as to why this was the case for the architect of this great American house.

Theodate Pope was an avidly bookish person. At the time she began seriously to consider architecture as a possible career, she wrote in her diary that she meant to read up on the subject.[8] The 1880s was an era of burgeoning scholarship on early American architecture. Among the volumes standing to this day on the library shelves at Hill-Stead are, not surprisingly, several from the period dedicated to the history of English Colonial and Georgian houses. Some volumes are technical; some, historical. All were popular works reflecting the taste of the time. Although some predate the design of Hill-Stead and some appeared later, all have an important place in our understanding of the design and meaning of the house.

Norman Isham and Albert F. Brown's *Early Rhode Island Houses*, of 1895, is there. Written by architects, it is a detailed analysis of the structural technology of seventeenth-century homes, illustrated by analytical drawings. Thomas Allen Glenn's two-volume *Some Colonial Mansions and Those Who Lived in Them*, published in 1899 and 1900, also occupies a shelf, having appeared just as Hill-Stead rose on its lofty site. The work of an historian, it is well illustrated with drawings and photographs. One photograph of the porticoed facade of Mount Vernon located on the Potomac River, from 1743, in Virigina, accompanied the chapter on the Washingtons and their house. Another photograph featured the entrance hall of Carter's Grove, in Virginia, the James River plantation of Carter Burwell, built in the Georgian style between 1750 and 1755. As his book's title makes clear, Glenn's focus—like that of Julius Gay in his volume on Farmington—is on the legendary inhabitants of these homes as much as on their architecture, and Glenn is careful to provide detailed genealogies of the families. Both the classical forms of the architecture and its association with distinguished ancestry must have caught Theodate's attention.

Now missing from the library shelves but well known to Theodate as she detailed Hill-Stead was a more academic work, *The Georgian Period*. This large collection of writings, measured drawings, and photographs devoted to English Colonial and American Federal architecture was edited by William Rotch Ware of

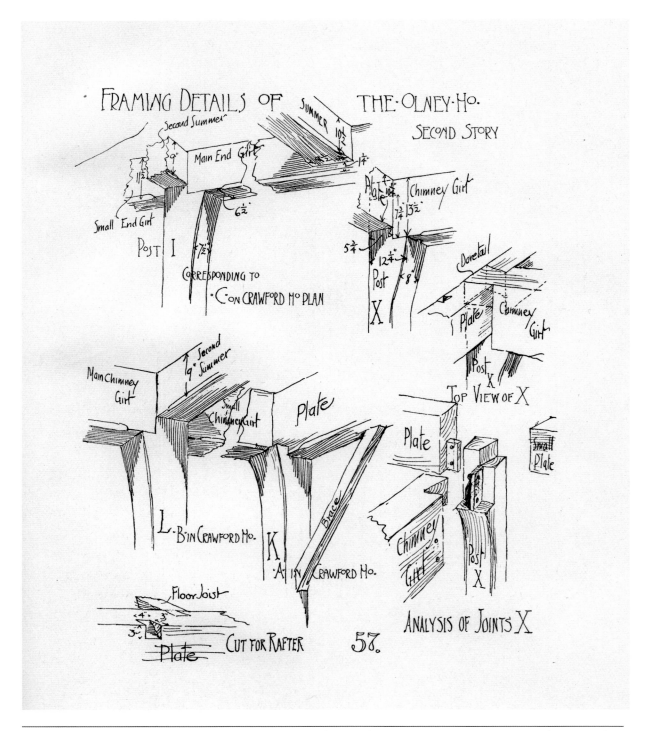

The Olney House, North Providence, early-eighteenth-century framing details. From Theodate Pope's copy of Norman Isham and Albert F. Brown, *Early Rhode Island Houses*, 1895.

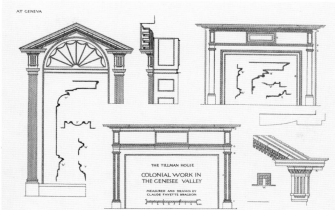

American Architect and Building News and published in seventeen large folios between 1898 and 1902. In December 1900, Theodate gave as a gift a set of the earlier folios to Richard F. Jones, her contractor and builder, remarking that "it would serve as a reminder of the many busy worried pleasant hours we had spent over the details of the house."[9] Like her contemporaries in established architectural offices, Theodate went to these books to ensure the authenticity of her Colonial and Federal details. The crisp line drawings in Ware's folios of fireplace frames, doorways, and assorted interior and exterior elements from Mount Vernon, Carter's Grove, and other early American sources came to life at Hill-Stead.

Another volume in the library at Hill-Stead picks up where these catalogues of forms leave off to suggest their meaning at the turn of the century. *American Renaissance*, written by a combative New Jersey architect named Joy Wheeler Dow, surveys domestic architecture in the United States around the turn of the century, condemning the excesses of the Victorian period while championing the restraint of the English Colonial and Federal works. It is illustrated with photographs of revival homes designed by the author and others. Dow's book is less history, however, than diatribe. Like other proponents of the Colonial- and Federal-era Revival, Dow was a zealot, proselytizing for an architecture expressive of conservative values.

In his discussion of the emergence of a Midwestern Prairie School around the figure of Frank Lloyd Wright (1867–1959), Dow castigated it as undomestic, rootless,

LEFT: Stairway in Main Hall, Carter's Grove. From Theodate Pope's copy of Thomas Allen Glenn, *Some Colonial Mansions and Those Who Lived in Them*, 1899–1900 RIGHT: Plate of interior details from *The Georgian Period* (1899–1902). Theodate Pope gave early folios of this authoritative publication to her builder, Richard F. Jones.

and foreign. He sneered at what he called a "newly-invented architecture" so strange that it was "simply impossible to prevail upon ancestral ghosts, legends and folk-lore, that habitually are part and parcel of the habitation of man, to have anything to do [with it]."[10] Although this may sound like an odd way to talk about buildings, beyond shelter, architecture sends messages, and Dow's message reflected a widely held attitude toward the revival of early American forms when Theodate Pope began her work at Hill-Stead.

Dow's tract first appeared in 1902 as a series of articles that were reissued in 1904 in the edition now at Hill-Stead. Therefore, it would not have been available until after the house was largely finished. The attitudes Dow expressed, however, were well known and shared by other revivalists. This fact is indispensable to an understanding of the assumptions upon which the Colonial- and Federal-era Revivals flourished around 1900 and of the symbolic basis upon which Theodate and her parents must have founded their Farmington residence. Dow's opening paragraphs declared the iconographic associative value of these forms in the well-conceived revival dwelling:

> *The house one builds must mean something besides artistic and engineering skill.*
> *It must presuppose, by subtle architectural expression, both in itself and in its*
> *surroundings, that its owner possessed, once upon a time, two good parents, four*
> *grandparents, eight great grand-parents, and so on; had, likely, brothers and sisters,*
> *uncles and aunts, all eminently respectable and endeared to him; that bienséance and*
> *family order have flourished in his line from time immemorial—there were no black*
> *sheep to make him ashamed—and that he has inherited heirlooms, plate, portraits,*
> *miniatures, pictures, rare volumes, diaries, letters and state archives to link him up*
> *properly in historical succession and progression. We are covetous of our niche in*
> *history. We want to belong somewhere and to something....We may not, indeed, have*
> *inherited the house we live in. We may not remember that either of our parents or any*
> *of our grandparents...ever gloried in the quiet possession of as ideal a homestead...but*
> *for the sake of goodness—for the sake of making the world appear a more decent place*
> *to live in—let us pretend that they did.*[11]

Reading this must have confirmed for Theodate Pope the rightness of her design for her parents' new house.

JANUARY 26, 1889 (AGE 21)

I AM QUITE INTERESTED IN PAPA'S SUGGESTION
OF MY STUDYING ARCHITECTURE.

FEBRUARY 18, 1889 (AGE 22)

HOW WOULD THE STUDIES OF PHILOSOPHY AND
ARCHITECTURE GO TOGETHER? THE STUDY
OF BOTH OUGHT TO MAKE MY MIND WELL
BALANCED.

LETTER TO WILLIAM RUTHERFORD MEAD
SEPTEMBER 17, 1898 (AGE 31)

I am writing for and in the interests of my father. We have now decided instead of having you submit sketches to us, to send you the plans that I have been working over at intervals for some years to draw to your scale and make an elevation of in the event of our coming to a mutual agreement. Consequently, as it is my plan, I expect to decide on all the details as well as all the more important questions of plan that may arise. That must be clearly understood at the outset, so as to save unnecessary friction in the future. In other words, it will be a Pope house instead of a McKim, Mead, and White.

If, after submitting my plans to you, you decide to undertake the work abiding by my conditions, please write me very explicitly just how you charge…In conclusion, I will say that I am not nearly as difficult to deal with as this would seem, for I am very tolerant of advice and always open to suggestions and good reasoning.

One can also hear in Dow's condemnation of Victorian work as pretentious and ugly Theodate's own words of 1900, on being tired "of seeing these flimsy highly colored hen houses"[12]. For Dow, only the revival residence, of which he designed many, would fit his aims. Traditional forms, he asserted, spoke reassuringly of the continuity of family, history, place, estate, propriety, and social order at the turn of the twentieth century, even if they projected an ideal vision of the past rather than its reality. The revival house took the curse off of new money. It conveyed ancestor worship and pride in genealogy. It was the proper style with which to express the Popes' deep New England roots.

If the ideal of expressing one's American roots through one's choice of architecture was especially strong at the turn of the twentieth century, this was particularly true in Connecticut. Across the country the older Anglo-Saxon population was confronted by the massive waves of immigrants from peripheral European countries such as Ireland, Poland, and southern Italy: immigrants who, for reasons of class, education, religion, language, or lifestyle were looked upon with disdain by the Yankee population. Those Americans like the Popes who traveled frequently to Europe to visit museums or to buy art and antiques did not associate with such people. Connecticut was an important destination for the "Polanders," the Slavic people who began to arrive there in the 1880s to work like slaves in the expanding tobacco fields of the Connecticut River Valley (and eventually came to own most of it).[13] They also arrived in Farmington itself to work in the neighborhood mills. A revival house could be seen as a deeply founded, reassuring bulwark against this foreign invasion.

The architecture of Hill-Stead is at once an outstanding and a canonical example of the Anglo-American revival: its creator, however, was anything but canonical. Theodate was an independent, determined, thirty-one-year-old woman when she focused on designing her parents' house. She had grown up in Cleveland society but rejected its expectation that she marry locally and well. Having studied at Miss Porter's School in Farmington, she eventually returned there to live on her own. Slowly her thoughts turned to a career in architecture, at a time when a female architect was most rare in this country. She became one of a pioneering group of women designers, born between the 1850s and the 1870s, that included Louise Blanchard Bethune, Katharine Cotheal Budd, Sophia Hayden, Mary Colter, Julia Morgan, and Eliza Newkirk Rogers. Unlike these trained architects, Theodate remained largely unschooled. She dreamed architectural dreams from an early age, and she spent hours putting her dreams on paper. She especially worked and reworked her project for an ideal farmstead—a project that would come to enhanced realization in Farmington.

Architecture was only one of Theodate Pope's intellectual passions, but it was one that was encouraged by her father from early in her life, and one she pursued, if not continuously, then with distinction. Theodate's education in this area began with trips abroad with her parents looking at paintings and buildings. She avoided training in an architect's office for, although she wrote that she "would not be satisfied" unless she "studied practically," she feared it would make her "rather mannish. And of all the unlovely things in the world an unwomanly woman is the worst."[15] Even if she had wanted to, it would have been difficult to break into the "old boys' club" that was then the architect's drafting room. Sophia Hayden graduated from the school of architecture at the Massachusetts Institute of Technology. Julia Morgan studied at the Ecole des Beaux-Arts in Paris. Some schools of architecture opened their doors to women by the 1880s: There is no record, however, that Theodate attempted to enter one.[16] Her only known related academic instruction stemmed from short periods in the mid-1890s studying art history, largely under the direction of Allan Marquand, the famed founder of the Department of Art and Archaeology at Princeton University and expert on the Della Robbia family of Italian Renaissance sculptors. For this reason, and also because she was a woman, untried, not an exceptionally skilled drafter (in a period when architectural draftsmanship had reached the status of high art), and was guided by her father to engage the help of the distinguished New York firm of McKim, Mead & White in the execution of the drawings for Hill-Stead, the idea that Theodate Pope was the architect of the house has, on occasion, been belittled. Nonetheless, study of the preserved information about the progress of the design affirms that the schema of Hill-Stead was hers and hers alone, in the same sense that buildings by celebrity architects like Daniel Burnham, H. H. Richardson, or Frank Gehry are theirs even though they have had the support of large office staffs and may not have made drawings themselves.

Some architects have been known to mentally picture an entire building before sitting down to draw it or before telling someone to lay it out. There is the famous story of Frank Lloyd Wright creating the complete design of Falling Water in his head before putting it on paper. H. H. Richardson also said he could design in this fashion. In his maturity he never drew anything other than thumbnail sketches—

"conceptual diagrams," as his biographer (and later, friend of Theodate) Marianna Van Rensselaer, called them. These were translated into architectural graphics by Richardson's assistants, who then signed the drawings with his name. Theodate had the same conceptual skill; it is said that, after pondering the project over time, she conceived the layout of her Avon Old Farms School in a flash of inspiration.[17]

An architect mentally formulates a design and then may draw it or may tell an assistant to draw it: in either case the person conceiving is the designer. From the beginning, Theodate's working method reflected that of other architects, as we can see, for example, from the sheet of preliminary drawings for the barn at Hill-Stead. The drawings are outline elevations on brown detail paper and were drafted in November 1898, probably by the carpenter-architect Henry Hall Mason, as guides for drawings to be made in the McKim, Mead & White office.[18] Theodate worked them over with extensive notes and rough sketches, demonstrating her impressive attention to detail both practical and aesthetic. In a note keyed to a section through the carriage shed, referring to its asymmetrical gable roof, for example, she cautions, "This pitch looks queer but it is just the way I want it." In another note, related to the south elevation, she again makes it clear that she has "intentionally drawn these roofs at different pitches." Other notes, on clapboards of alternating width, shingles, hand-wrought hinges, rafters, and so on, demonstrate her complete control of the design. Her question, "Is the [laundry] chimney too near barn for safety?" is even more important, especially in light of the fact that a fire later destroyed one unit of the barn. A brick fire wall was erected to reduce that danger.

In another instance, Theodate sent a drafted detail of the plan of the front entry to the McKim firm asking for advice.[19] This seems to be an overlay of a drawing from that office, corrected and annotated. Surviving drawings from the office of H. H. Richardson show the same characteristics: rough plans drawn to scale by a draftsman are scrubbed over with notes and thumbnail sketches by the principal. The process was repeated until the design satisfied the boss. Theodate was to follow this common method throughout her architectural career.

Architectural production is a matter of teamwork, but there is usually just one leader. Theodate hired drafters but directed their pencils. When she first approached the office of McKim, Mead & White, she knew what she wanted to achieve but needed help to achieve it, just as Frank Gehry needs engineers to realize his computer-generated fantasies. She worked with neither of the celebrated designing partners,

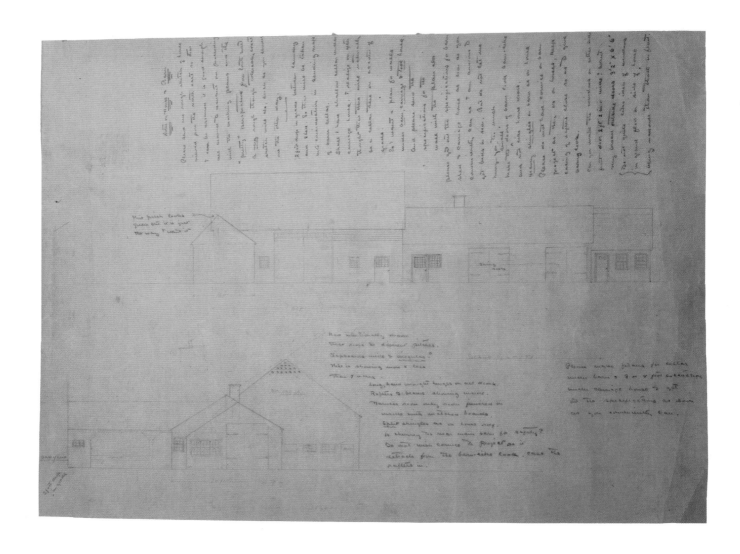

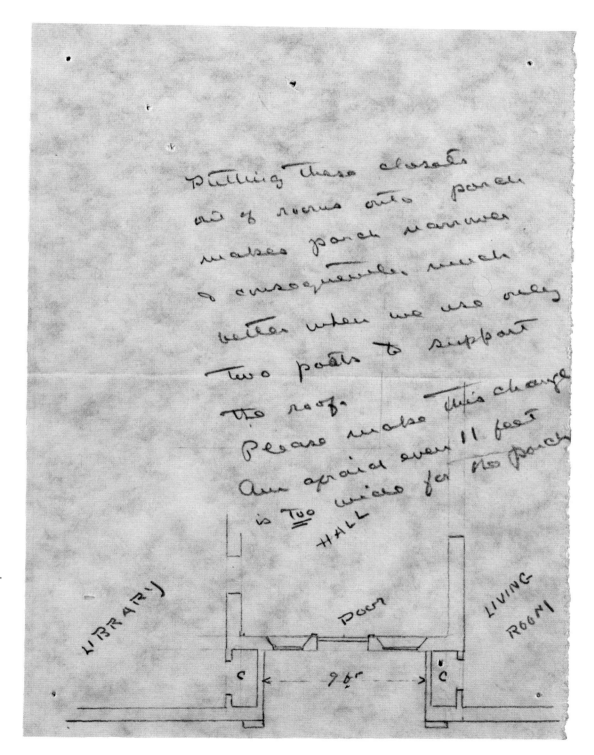

Hill-Stead, elevations of carriage barn, 1898. Drawn by Henry Hall Mason with extensive notes by Theodate Pope.

Preliminary plan of the Entry Hall with notes in Theodate Pope's hand

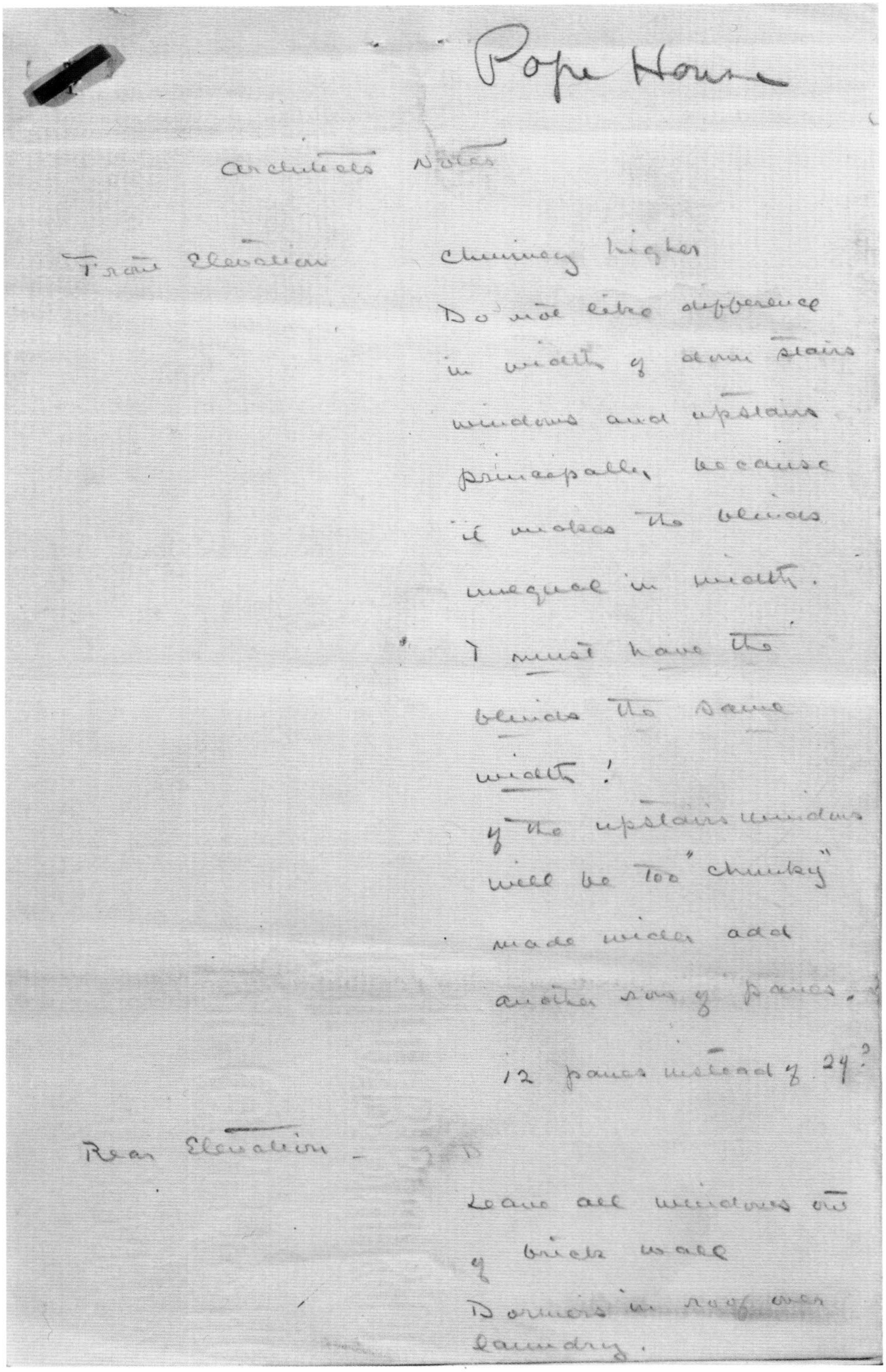

Pope House

Architects Notes

Front Elevation

Chimney higher
Do not like difference
in width of down stairs
windows and upstairs
principally, because
it makes the blinds
unequal in width.
I *must* have the
blinds the same
width !
If the upstairs windows
will be too "chunky"
made wider add
another row of panes.
12 panes instead of 24?

Rear Elevation —

Leave all windows out
of brick wall
Dormers in roof over
laundry.

Undated memo with
architectural notes written by
Theodate Pope for McKim,
Mead & White

Charles Follen McKim or Stanford White. She consulted with William Rutherford Mead, whose time, according to a student of the firm, was taken up with supervising the office and so "had little left for designing."[20] Mead eventually assigned Theodate's project to Egerton Swartwout, who would later become well known but was then a junior draftsman. Subsequently, the project was reassigned to the little-remembered Walter R. Wilder. These draftsmen helped with details, but essentially Theodate used their pencils to draft her dream. When she did not like something on plans or elevations she received, she sent the drawings back to New York for correction. There survive, for example, sheets from her hand of "Architect's Notes," "Masons Notes," "Waterproofing Notes," and "Notes on house elevations," in addition to a sheet of very rough sketches that contain her memos about design changes to be forwarded to the McKim office. As we have seen, the fire wall between the laundry and the barn was built in answer to a query from her. It was she who supervised at the site every detail of the execution of the drawings, a fact that led to a reduced fee for the McKim office.[21]

It was Theodate's father who sent her to the architects in New York. As president of the National Malleable Castings Company of Cleveland, he knew many architects and builders. His close friend J. H. Whittemore had a house designed by Stanford White in nearby Naugatuck, Connecticut, and recommended the firm. (Whittemore would eventually become a major client of the firm.) McKim, Mead & White was one of the premier proponents of the Anglo-American revival, but in 1898 Theodate herself was no newcomer to the style. Not only had she studied publications on colonial building, such as the Isham and Brown volume mentioned earlier, but throughout the 1890s she had been learning firsthand, studying "practically" the design and construction methods of preexisting buildings as she directed the rehabilitation, redecoration, and ultimately augmentation of her first Farmington home. Located at the bottom of the slope upon which Hill-Stead eventually rose was an eighteenth-century center-chimney saltbox she named "The O'Rourkery" (after the previous owner, James O'Rourke). She later added to it a second historic building she called "The Gundy," thus creating an additive composition of colonial work and anticipating on a small scale her approach to the massing of Hill-Stead.

Such hands-on experience equals, if not exceeds, academic training. Theodate was aided in this project, first by Henry Hall Mason, a local builder-architect who, as we have seen, would later work at Hill-Stead, and then by the architect Melvin H. Hapgood of Hartford, who designed in the "Old Colonial" style. Sarah Porter, the founder of the school Theodate had attended, hailed the result "an exact duplication of the farmhouse of eighty years ago." The house also won praise from the publishers of *Farmington, Connecticut: The Village of Beautiful Homes* as being in "perfect keeping with the customs of the times in which the house was built."[22] Theodate's work at the O'Rourkery caused J. H. Whittemore to exclaim in 1896, "It is evident you do not need the professional services of anybody."[23] Although the statement was made in reference to an arboreal problem described by Theodate, it clearly had wider implications. Two years later she was ready to tackle a much larger project in a retrospective vein—her parents' house up the hill.

From the time of Pliny the Younger (61–121) if not before, people have sought relief from the pressures of urban life in a villa, chateau, dacha, or country house.[24] Hill-Stead was created in the bucolic Connecticut River Valley as a foil to the Pope family's urban setting in Cleveland. The style of the Euclid Avenue home stood in contrast to that of Hill-Stead. The Boston architect William Ralph Emerson (1833–1917) designed the former in 1883, while at the peak of his career. The architect's pen and ink perspective drawing, as well as photographs taken in 1913, show it to have been a fashionable brick Romanesque Revival design with Queen Anne details and William Morris–style furnishings. A dark house, hemmed in by neighbors, its character was harsh, and Theodate disliked it.[25] Genteel Hill-Stead was her answer. That Alfred Pope, a man with much experience working with architects and builders, had his troubles with Emerson may have inclined him to give Theodate her chance at Farmington. He believed in her abilities, even as he knew she was a person who followed her own mind.

In the summer of 1898 Theodate first wrote to the firm of McKim, Mead & White to introduce herself and to request drawings for the house to be built in Farmington.[26] She described the site and outlined the program; she also asked for a "beautifully planned house" but no elevations. On 5 September her father advised her to send her own plan for the house to the McKim office, asking them instead for help with "minor details" of construction.[27] The reason for the change can be found in Theodate's letter of 17 September to the firm, in which she tells Mead that she had not answered his letter of some three months earlier because she had learned that charge of the house "was to be in the hands of a very young man."[28] She and her father no longer wanted a plan by the firm if it was to be done by an inexperienced draftsman, she wrote, but were sending to the office a design that Theodate had been

The original building of The O'Rourkery, so named by Theodate Pope as she bought the house from Mr. James O'Rourke in 1892, dates back to ca. 1725. Theodate and a friend sit in the open doorway.

The O'Rourkery, Keeping Room. Theodate Pope began her career as an architect restoring this eighteenth-century house for her own use.

"working over at intervals for some years to draw to your scale and make an elevation of in the event of our coming to a mutual agreement."[29] Impatient, on 29 September she wrote to the firm again, explaining that she was "anxiously awaiting an answer" to her letter, asking if Mead was away, and requesting that her letter and the "role of plans I sent him at the same time" be forwarded to him.[30]

Theodate's earliest drawings for her ideal farmhouse no longer survive, but there is preserved one small, rough outline of the plan of the final layout of Hill-Stead, including overall dimensions of the main block, wings, service tail, and barn, drawn on the reverse of a letter from her father dated 19 September 1898. It seems to be the earliest visualization of the house that has survived, and it is just the kind of preliminary thumbnail sketch, or "conceptual diagram," so familiar from H. H. Richardson's and other architects' working method. This is the Pope house in embryo.

Theodate's letter of 17 September continued, "as it is my plan, I expect to decide in all the details as well as all more important questions of plan that may arise. This must be clearly understood at the outset....In other words, it will be a Pope house instead of a McKim, Mead, and White [one]." She realized this was a marked departure from her first proposal, as well as a presumptuous demand from one so professionally inexperienced, and so concedes, "naturally, you could not without seeing the plans agree to this, as it seems a real risk of the very deserved reputation your Firm holds." She concluded, once the deal was made, "the work could be turned over

Alfred and Ada Pope Residence, Cleveland, Ohio, drawing by architect William Ralph Emerson, 1883–84

[543]

Florence Sept 19

Dear Theodate

I hardly know what to write you. We have not had any letter from you for some time to act as a stimulant. I have about exhausted my plans in imagination in telling you thoughts about the new place and suggesting how to proceed in "breaking ground"—

We are enjoying Italy or I am more than anticipated. I find I have grown. My taste is more Catholic and I see more— You

---

Theodate Pope's initial conception of Hill-Stead house and barn sketched on the back of a letter from her father. The rough drawing is remarkably close to the plan as realized.

to someone in your office who has more experience and is very solid on construction."

It is often speculated that the McKim office took on this work as a favor to Alfred Pope's good friend J. H. Whittemore. It is also true, however, that architects need to keep their people busy and often accept drafting jobs as well as design commissions in order to ensure a steady flow of cash into the office. Theodate Pope was the architect of Hill-Stead.

> *[it] is to be frame—one very large living room very large dining room also a study and bedroom and little sitting room—the last two connected, then pantrys kitchen scullery and laundry all on ground floor. Do what you can for nice guest rooms upstairs besides the servants rooms have two guest rooms with baths connecting also a general bath room and one connected with the first floor bed room.*[31]

Her "Do what you can" quickly became, "Do it my way," as Theodate introduced her own plan and gradually took control of all aspects of the project.

Construction began with the barn late in 1898. An all-but-definitive set of drawings for the main house from the McKim, Mead & White office dated September 1899 details Theodate's original program. The drawings show that the Entry Hall on the first floor, corresponding to the central feature of a Georgian symmetrical plan, is surrounded by asymmetrical arrangements of rooms zoned by usage. Open to the right are the reception rooms: the Drawing Room with its smaller Ell Sitting Room, fronted by a portico, and, to the rear, the Dining Room. To the left are more private spaces: the Library; the Office, fronted by another portico (this would change in the later remodeling); and a Parlor Bed or Retiring Room. Beyond the Dining Room stretches the wing with the Kitchen and other service areas. The asymmetrical arrangement of the front rooms is reinforced by the presence of unaligned polygonal bays extending the Drawing Room and the Office.

Theodate designed the interior of Hill-Stead as the appropriate setting for her parents' style of living. This was a household attended by a large number of "help," including the long-serving butler Earnest Bohlen (1853–1942). The members of the Pope family lived, even in their country house, according to the expectations of decorum associated with the elevated economic class to which they belonged. The communal areas were not for lounging but were formal reception rooms where friends from near and far, such as Mary Cassatt or Henry James, were entertained

LETTER TO MR. SWARTWOUT OF MCKIM, MEAD & WHITE

CA. 1899 (AGE 32)

There are several things in regard to the house plans I wish to speak of. Please see that the upper and lower sash do not meet at a height in the window that would be on a line with ones eyes in looking out. That is raise or lower the window to the right height. Of course there is a difference in height of people but it must be right for father and he is 5'11" tall.

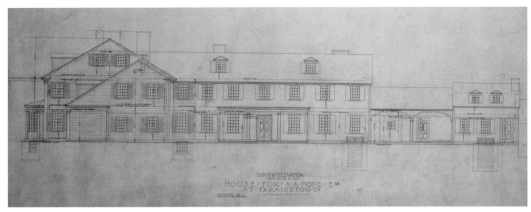

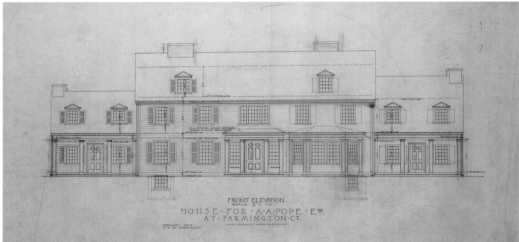

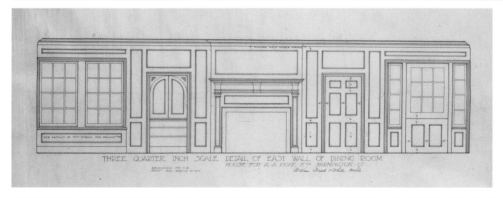

TOP: Hill-Stead, South Elevation, McKim, Mead & White Architects, drawing by Egerton Swartwout, 1899 MIDDLE: Hill-Stead, Front Elevation, McKim, Mead & White Architects, drawing by Egerton Swartwout, 1899 BOTTOM: Hill-Stead, detail of East Wall, Dining Room, McKim, Mead & White Architects, drawing by W. R. Wilder, 1899

beneath some of the most important recent works of art to be found in this country. Even when the family dined alone, its members "dressed" formally and assembled in the large Dining Room. The recreation of Georgian Colonial interiors, punctuated by modern paintings, set the stage for the pattern of cultured domestic life at Hill-Stead.

Some of the architectural features of the interior seem inspired by Alfred Pope's letters to his daughter near the beginning of the design process. He sent much advice to Theodate during the course of the project. In one letter, after saying "I don't care to direct details," he proceeds to do just that:

> *[T]he large living room would be better with a mantel....I like fireplaces in the important bedrooms....I am satisfied with plan to grain the woodwork down stairs except possibly the large living room and wing [the adjoining Ell Sitting Room]. It seems to me that in an 1830 house such rooms were dignified by being plain color or white.*[32]

He then adds "I don't like to say white," apparently remembering that it was not a common color for Georgian or Federal houses.

As the early American styles were very popular at the turn of the twentieth century, it was possible to order interior details—trim, fireplace frames, moldings, and the like—from large suppliers. The interiors of the main first-floor rooms at Hill-Stead were inspired by Theodate's and her builder's perusal of the illustrations in books such as Thomas Allen Glenn's *Some Colonial Mansions* and especially the earlier folios of The *Georgian Period*, which were drawn in the McKim office and custom made by William H. Jackson & Company of New York.[33] They echoed those of the early nineteenth century, with fireplace frames, for example, of paneled Doric pilasters supporting the cornice and mantel painted or faux-grained to match the finish of the surrounding trim. Theodate's attention to details here is characteristic of all her work.

The west, or principal, elevation from the 1899 set of drawings shows the exterior of the main block embraced by lower wings housing the Office and the Ell Sitting Room off the Drawing Room. The house rose from these drawings as a loosely arranged conglomeration of white clapboarded forms with dark green accents. The western elevation itself reads as symmetrical at first glance, until one notices the unbalanced placement of the Drawing Room bay to the right of the entry and the higher ridge of the right wing. An orthodox classicist would condemn this as the work of an amateur, but it seems a knowing part of the program to create the effect of a house that grew over time. It also recognizes the fact that a building, and especially this house, is never seen as an orthogonal, or frontal, elevation, and that an angled view will distort symmetry anyway.

Since the house was to be approached by vehicular traffic from the southwest, from Mountain Road, along the curvilinear drive lined with stone walls, the 1899 south elevation, showing the main block of the residence and the service wing stretching to the Laundry Room and Butler's Quarters on the east, became as important as the west front. The schema of continuous architecture announces itself here. In this drawing the Carriage Porch has yet to receive its arcaded approach, and the reception area serving Kitchen and Laundry (now enclosed and called the Stone Porch) is fronted by a pair of open three-centered arches. As we shall see, the proximity of carriage and service entrances separated only by the highly visible Kitchen is a troublesome aspect of Theodate's plan.

With the cellar dug and working drawings prepared, Theodate gave Swartwout permission to produce a "pretty perspective" of the house from the southwest as she wanted to show it to her parents.[34] In selecting this view—the view a visitor first sees when approaching the house along the carefully designed drive from Mountain Road—she obviously wanted to emphasize the asymmetrical, picturesque character of the composition, including the saltbox silhouette of the wing housing the Ell Sitting Room off the Drawing Room. In this period even established architects called upon professional "perspectivists" to create eye-catching views of prospective buildings. Swartwout's view of Hill-Stead depicts the house and barn as a set of loosely connected, articulated shapes set into the landscape. Had the western front been left as shown in this drawing, or even with the addition of the Drawing Room bay, the central dormer, and the extended Carriage Porch—all of which are lacking here but had appeared by the end of the first building campaign—the house would have had more the look of a rambling farmhouse than it has now. The addition of the Mount Vernon–style portico pulls some of these elements together.

During construction in March 1901, Theodate visited George Washington's home in Virginia.[35] She may have known it previously from the illustrations in Glenn's *Colonial Mansions* or *The Georgian Period*, as views of the Potomac front of that national shrine were published in both. She must have felt some connection to the place, for it had been preserved (and is still administered) largely by women under the

rubric of the Mount Vernon Ladies Association. (In 1901 Theodate became a member of the Colonial Dames of America, another organization dedicated to the preservation of early American architecture.) In October 1901 she wrote in her diary that William Mead had come "to help us with suggestions about the porch we are going to put across the front of the house."[36] Just what he may have suggested remains unknown. Because Mount Vernon is wider than the main block at Hill-Stead, Theodate included only six of Mount Vernon's eight colossal piers, but she kept the Chinese Chippendale railings installed after Washington's death that were prominent in the views in the books in her library. The railings were removed from the portico at Mount Vernon in 1936. The Mount Vernon–style portico at Hill-Stead added a touch of Southern neo-Federal pomp to the New England Colonial hominess of the first conception.

By 1901 the house was ready for occupancy, but changes made in 1906 brought it to the architectural arrangement we know today—changes that indicate that Theodate continued to rethink her design even after the initial building campaign had come to an end. On the north a temple-form porch supported by piers now extended off a new Office for Mr. Pope (presently called the Morning Room).[37] It added another asymmetrical element to the house when seen from the west. The addition of what is now called the Second Library replaced the original Office and included a polygonal bay window that took the place of the old office portico. Although it echoed the Drawing Room bay (both are crowned with the Mount Vernon

First rendering of Hill-Stead house and barn, McKim, Mead & White Architects, drawing by Egerton Swartwout, 1899

Theodate Pope at George
Washington's home, Mount
Vernon, Virginia, 1901

JUNE 20, 1901 (AGE 34)

THIS HOME SEEMS STRANGELY UNREAL TO ME.
I FEEL AS IF I WERE WALKING IN A DREAM AND
NOT IN FARMINGTON. IT ALL SEEMS SO UNLIKE
THE FARMINGTON I HAVE ALWAYS KNOWN, EVERY
THING UP HERE, BUT IT IS ALL SO VERY RESTFUL
AND BEAUTIFUL. I FEEL SO AT PEACE WITH THE
ACCOMPLISHMENT OF IT. I THINK ONE OF THE
STRANGEST THINGS ABOUT IT ALL IS TO SEE
ERNEST SERVING US HERE——IN FARMINGTON——
THAT SEEMS SO CHIMERICAL I FEEL AS IF
THE WHOLE THING WOULD DISAPPEAR LIKE A
DISSOLVING VIEW. I GO AROUND IN A DAZE AND
FEEL AS IF I WERE TREADING AIR.

ABOVE: Early photograph of Hill-Stead, ca. 1901. Note the portico and covered walkway have not yet been added.

LEFT: Undated note from Theodate Pope presumably to Egerton Swartwout asking that he be sure to get the details right on an important drawing they will eventually share with her parents

Before drawing the important perspective of house for father & mother please be sure of all details so that general effect will be right. But if you do it yourself as I hope you will, you will know just what I meant.

T.A.P.

In 1906, the house was enlarged and a Second Library and Office were added. The original west facing porch was redesigned as a second polygonal bay. The temple-form North Porch added new character to this elevation.

Chippendale-style railing), it did not enhance the symmetry of the front facade. Its face aligns with the front wall of the house, whereas the Drawing Room bay juts forward from that line, and, more importantly, it is exposed to the elements whereas the Drawing Room bay is sheltered by the portico. The end result visually enhances the unorthodox main facade of Hill-Stead while it energizes it. The middle point between the bay windows is offset to the left from the axis of the main block, and that produces a kind of double schema for the composition. Even at its most formal, the elevation remains informal, carrying on the lively irregularity that guided the shaping of the entire house. Perhaps it can be said that it is the perfect reflection of the unorthodoxy of its architect.

The contrast between New England informality and Georgian or Federal formality is built into the approaches. Given its location away from the center of Farmington, the visitor who arrived in a carriage or, later, by automobile, first saw the house from the southwest. To reach the formal entry hall beneath the Mount Vernon portico on the west facade, the visitor needed to circumvent the corner of the house on foot and was thus forced to view the main facade at a sharp angle. (Another, less well-traveled approach to the house, by foot up the slope from the O'Rourkery, puts the visitor directly in front of the portico.)

The more convenient entry is on the south, marked by the covered approach or walkway. After entering the Carriage Porch, one turns left to enter, rather

LEFT: Alfred, Ada and Theodate Pope at Hill-Stead, ca. 1902 RIGHT: Guests arriving at Hill-Stead's Carriage Porch, ca. 1902. Photograph by Theodate Pope.

awkwardly, one corner of the Dining Room. It is surprising to find this kind of back-door guest entrance in a house of Hill-Stead's pretensions. Even more surprising is the direct access provided by the same approach to the Kitchen and service entrance to the house: access that rightly disturbs the critics, for it violates the basic assumption about classical architectural hierarchy—that public and private, ceremony and service, should be clearly separated.[38] In the (translated) words of the Italian Renaissance master Andrea Palladio, "we ought to put the principal and considerable parts [of a building] in places [that are] the most seen, and the less beautiful, in places as much hidden from the eye as possible... [so that they do not] in any measure render the more beautiful parts disagreeable."[39]

The arcaded approach to the Carriage Porch seems to have been an afterthought (it is not on the original plan), clearly intended to distinguish the visitors' entry from the service porch. For some, the layout of this part of the plan seems to be unresolved and to reflect Theodate's immaturity as a designer; for others, it merely stems from the (admittedly, here, only slightly) unbuttoned rules of country living. The entire problem may be the result of Theodate's desire to show her house to vehicular visitors first at the angle from the southwest, at the same time that she wanted not to run the drive in front of the west portico.

However the visitor reaches the formal entrance in the center of the west facade, he or she finds a massive two-part Dutch door that opens into the Entry Hall with its staircase sweeping up to the second floor and a glimpse into the formal Dining Room (when the door is open). The overall form of the staircase was inspired by that at Carter's Grove in Virginia, as illustrated in Theodate's copy of Glenn's *Some Colonial Mansions*, although in a nod to simplicity the balusters are not turned as in the original. Theodate may have known similar rectangular balusters on the stair at Woodlawn in Virginia, as published in *The Georgian Period*.[40]

Left and right from the Entry Hall deep vistas open to view. To the right, one sees a receding prospect across the Drawing Room into the Ell Sitting Room, a prospect framed by a Georgian three-centered archway also reminiscent of that at Carter's Grove. That the relationship of staircase and archway here is altered from the one in Virginia shows Theodate's creative manipulation of sources. To the left, through a narrower doorway (closable when privacy was desired), the view extends across the two libraries toward the Office. The classical detailing of the interior woodwork was inspired by Theodate's reference books, but the ceilings are relatively

Entry Hall, *American Homes and Gardens*, February 1910

View from Drawing Room into Entry Hall

JULY 20, 1901 (AGE 34)

THE BURNING QUESTION IS, SUNDAY——GOLF OR
NOT? I AM FOR, FATHER AGAINST.

I CAN NOW SAY WE ARE LEADING THE LIFE
I HAVE MEANT WE SHOULD IF IT WAS EVER
POSSIBLE. A LARGE SIMPLE HOME TO RECEIVE
OUR GUESTS IN——AND THE RIGHT KIND OF
GUESTS AND LEISURE TO <u>LIVE</u> IN. GOD GRANT US
MANY YEARS OF IT, AND GRANT ME PERSONALLY
A CLEAR UNDERSTANDING AND THE POWER TO
DO RIGHT. I WANT MY HEAD IN THE SPIRITUAL
WORLD AND MY HANDS IN THIS ONE TO HELP
OTHERS.

MARCH 11, 1915 (AGE 48)

Mr. Howe, one of the editors of Town and Country, *came into my office the other day. He had been sent by Mr. Charles A. Platt, the architect, whom he said was an admirer of my work. Mr. Howe came with the idea of finding something he could publish in his paper. When he saw the colored rendering of Harris' school [Hop Brook School, Naugatuck, Conn.], which had just been returned to me from the exhibition, he said, "Bully! Bully! Bully!" and delighted me by understanding every point in the design. He told me that when it was built he wished to have photographs of it for reproduction. He also asked me if I would get busy having photographs taken of the Locust Valley house as he would be very pleased to use that and write it up.*

Did I tell you of the Nugent Publishing Company which requested my photograph for publication in a book of prominent New York architects they are getting out? You will be most amused to know that I was called up by telephone from their office and a masculine voice at the other end asked incredulously if I were really Theodate Pope the architect, and when I said I truly was, this voice apologetically explained that it would be impossible for them to use my photograph as they had just heard I was a woman. They had not believed the rumor, hence the incredulous voice over the telephone. So you see, although art has no sex, I am discriminated against, though on the merits of my work they had selected me as one of the architects whom they wished to mention.

low, and that scales down the space and emphasizes the horizontal sweep of the vistas through the interior. Their openness rivals anything achieved by the contemporary Midwestern Prairie School houses of Frank Lloyd Wright and his followers.

Hill-Stead quickly proved to be a favorite with the national architectural press. As early as November 1902 it appeared, attributed to McKim, Mead & White, in ten photographs in *The Architectural Review*. In August 1906 *The Architectural Record* published an equal number of photos, along with the attribution to the McKim office. Captions were the only text, and they dwelt primarily on the concordance between architecture and furnishings. In February 1910 Barr Ferree sought to put the house into its proper context in his article in *American Homes and Gardens*. He found it suitable for its historical environment, calling it "precisely the kind of house one would naturally look for in Farmington."[41] He characterized its design as a grouping of various parts from various structures, but called it a harmonious one, "with detailing of the most careful kind, a house that is at once scholarly and refined, modern and old."[42] That combination, he thought, was difficult to achieve, and "it has seldom been done so well" as at Hill-Stead.[43] Perhaps for the first time in print Theodate's presence is mentioned along with that of the McKim office, but only to say that the firm's work was "supplemented with the zealous assistance of Miss Pope, to whom much of the interior treatment is due."[44] As we have seen, the record demonstrates more than that. Interior decoration could be thought of as appropriate woman's work. It would have been unthinkable to give equal or major billing for more of the design to an unknown woman next to one of the most celebrated architectural firms of the day. Theodate would over time erase the "unknown," if not the "woman."

The remodeling of the O'Rourkery and the design of Hill-Stead marked the beginning of Theodate's career as an architect. In September 1900 she wrote in her diary that her "interest in architecture had always been more intense than my interest in any other art…If I only knew how to help the cause of good architecture!"[45] Several weeks later, in early December, she was self-assured enough in her aesthetic judgment to do just that, to criticize "very severely" the design of a house for her friend Harris Whittemore. The plan was good, she wrote, "but the exterior was inexpressibly ugly."[46] She also noted, "It may result in his having new elevation drawn."[47] Her career was launched.

Theodate opened an architectural office in New York in 1907. The state recognized her as a professional when she was licensed in 1916, and in 1933

Connecticut followed suit. She was elected to the American Institute of Architects in 1918. As a pioneering female architect, and one not required to work for a living, her list of realized buildings is not long, but it is choice, and punctuated with designs admired by the severest critics: her fellow architects.[48] The oeuvre, nearly all of which is located in Connecticut, consists largely of schools and houses, building types easily associated with female endeavors.

Hill-Stead was barely complete when Theodate set about designing a boarding school for girls called Westover in Middlebury, Connecticut. The plan is wrapped around an arcaded quadrangle; the style, again, is English Colonial, with echoes of contemporary British Arts and Crafts design. The front block is capped by a tall roof (that was to became something of a signature in her work), centered on a salient crowned by a triangular pediment and topped by a cupola. Two projecting wings embrace the facade: one that houses the chapel, and one that contains the headmistress's house. Although similar in size, the wings are articulated differently. Famed architect Cass Gilbert called Westover "beautifully designed and beautifully planned," and it has recently been labeled one of the best buildings in Connecticut by another informed admirer.[49] Hop Brook School in Naugatuck was designed in 1914, accepted for the American Architectural League exhibition the following year, and published in *Architecture* three years later.

Avon Old Farms School, begun in 1918, is the product of Theodate's pedagogical as well as architectural philosophy; like Thomas Jefferson at the University of Virginia, she devised the school's curriculum as well as supplied its accommodations. Her designs were inspired by the architecture of the Cotswolds in England, combined with English Arts and Crafts preindustrial forms. She would permit no modern methods of construction; wood and stone were cut and quarried on the site and were put into place by hand labor using ancient tools. Avon Old Farms School was also much published and justly celebrated by major architects such as Gilbert, Charles Platt, and, in our own day, Robert A. M. Stern.[50]

After Hill-Stead, Theodate's domestic architecture leaned toward the work of contemporary British designers such as Charles F. Annesley Voysey and Charles Rennie Mackintosh. Her "Red Room" at Westover parallels Mackintosh's work in Glasgow. Her Chamberlain house in Middlebury, Connecticut, of 1911, her Gates (or "Dormer") house of 1913 on Long Island, and the row of cottages she designed for her staff in Farmington in 1914 all take on British or Anglo-American characteristics.

LEFT: Chamberlain House, Middlebury, Conn., 1911   RIGHT: Avon Old Farms School, Avon, Conn., opened 1927

These are important, if far too little known, exemplars of early twentieth-century American domestic architecture.

Theodate Pope's biography and lack of formal training do not fit easily into the traditional pattern of the professional architect of the early twentieth century. That makes her achievement all the more noteworthy and none the less real. Many an architect has had to wait for years of experience to accomplish work of the personality, quality, and importance that she saw rise from her ideas on the knoll at Farmington. The occasion of the commission was a favorable one to be sure, coming from a doting father with the means to indulge his beloved daughter, but she rose wonderfully to that occasion. Hill-Stead is as fine a domestic architectural achievement of its period as any residential work by her more lauded male colleagues.[51]

THE FURNISHINGS *Edward S. Cooke, Jr.*

PRAISED RIGHT FROM THE BEGINNING as charming and dignified, Hill-Stead's refined combination of art, antiques, and historically inspired architecture continues to draw visitors intent on experiencing what Henry James described as "the momentary effect of a large slippery sweet inserted without warning" and celebrated as the sharpest "proof of the sovereign power of art."[1] However, it is important to recognize that the interiors the visitor sees today comprise more than a century of accumulation, subtraction, relocation, and refurbishment. Domestic furnishings such as textiles and wallpaper can be vulnerable to wear. Furniture, ceramics, small personal objects, and even paintings can migrate from one room to another or be discarded altogether in favor of something else. Certainly much that is original remains within Hill-Stead, which was designed in 1898 and constructed between 1899 and 1901. But to gain real insight into the initial conception of the house's furnishing philosophy it is essential to understand who took the initiative, who the suppliers were, and how the objects were brought together to create a specific look. In many ways Hill-Stead represents an important shift to a historically oriented philosophy that was knit together with an artistic vision. As such, it distinguishes itself as neither a fashionable "House Beautiful" of the 1880s nor a nostalgic Colonial Revival country house of the 1920s.

The decorative philosophy of the home that Alfred Atmore Pope (1842–1913) and Ada Brooks Pope (1844–1920) built in Cleveland between 1883 and 1885, fifteen years before moving to Farmington, provides an important context for understanding Hill-Stead. Designed by William Ralph Emerson (1833–1917), a Boston architect who gained particular fame for his work in the Shingle Style during the 1880s, their mansion at 949 Euclid Avenue featured interiors in

A quiet corner in the Ell Sitting Room illustrates the diversity of interior design elements at Hill-Stead. The painting *Peace*, Pierre Puvis de Chavannes (ca. 1861), hangs above the desk.

the latest fashion, as espoused by New York art critic Clarence Cook (1828–1900) in *The House Beautiful.*[2] In the Dining Room, furniture in a hybrid of Federal Revival and Arts and Crafts styles was surrounded by elaborately paneled wainscoting surmounted by floral wallpaper inspired by English designer William Morris and, above, by a large patterned wallpaper on the frieze and ceiling. Morris & Company papers and carpets had just been well received at the 1883 Foreign Fair in Boston, and Emerson would have been aware of their fashionability.[3] Along the walls, prints and paintings were spaced relatively far apart and a few choice objects were displayed on the sideboard, all in keeping with Cook's admonition to choose just a few beautiful objects rather than overpopulating walls or display surfaces.[4]

In the Parlor, a fireplace with tiled surround, ample mantel display space, and an architectural presence provided what Cook celebrated as "the spiritual and intellectual center of family life."[5] Other artistic touches included more Morris-inspired floral wallpaper, a papered ceiling with wooden moldings providing geometric designs, revival-style furniture, and a curtain-fronted midheight bookcase along one wall, upon the top of which were displayed decorative items such as plates and vases. The Library off of the hall was designed as the ultimate aesthetic space: the heavy joists, self-consciously tooled surfaces, built-in cupboard with bull's-eye glass front, and frieze carved with a motto all recall the British Arts and Crafts movement, an interest in which Emerson shared with prominent nineteenth-century American architect H. H. Richardson (1838–1886). The brick fireplace—replete with an extra display niche below the mantel and a shiny metal grate, andirons, and fireplace tools—anchored this room just as the tiled example did the Parlor.

For much of the interior furnishing of the Euclid Avenue home, the Popes seem to have relied upon a firm that offered full furniture, upholstery, and decorating services. In the last quarter of the nineteenth century, many industrial capitalists such as Alfred Pope turned to such custom furniture firms to oversee tasteful, fashionable decoration.[6] The likely candidate for the Pope home would be A. H. Davenport in Cambridge, Massachusetts, who worked closely with Richardson and offered Morris papers and textiles for sale. In a letter written about 1920 to her mother's secretary, Mr. F. Swenston, about the contents of Hill-Stead, the Popes' daughter, Theodate, (1867–1946), recounted that "much of the furniture is a reproduction of old designs and a great deal of that was brought on from our Cleveland house when we moved—having been made by Davenport in Boston."[7] Most of the wall treatments, area rugs,

lighting devices, and furniture seem to be standard stock for the fashionable market of this period. One of the few more personal touches was the incorporation of a few single pieces of antique, or more accurately, revival furniture such as Windsor and Chippendale-style chairs in the Library; but such accent pieces were in keeping with Cook's principles.

Whereas the Popes turned to a decorating firm in fitting out the Euclid Avenue home, Theodate took a different approach when, in the summer of 1890, she rented a mid-eighteenth-century house in Farmington, which she named the O'Rourkery. She immediately cleaned the house, installed a furnace, and set about decorating each room with appropriate period colors, wallpapers, furniture, and accessories.[8] Responding to the historical context, she hunted for local antiques and assembled coastal Connecticut turned chairs, flag-seated vernacular New England Chippendale chairs, candlestands, plank-seated Windsor chairs, fourposter bedsteads, maple fancy chairs, painted toleware, tall case clocks, English creamware, pewter, and old fireplace equipment. It is telling that a 1902 photograph of Theodate placed her in a rocking chair in front of a cooking fireplace, complete with trammel and hot water kettle.

The adornment of the walls with historic prints underscored the decorating theme. After a visit to the O'Rourkery by Miss Porter's School headmistress Sarah Porter, Theodate wrote, years later in her memoirs, that Miss Porter found her house

LEFT: Dining Room RIGHT: Library, Alfred and Ada Pope Residence, 949 Euclid Avenue, Cleveland, Ohio, built between 1883–85

Theodate Pope at Keeping Room
fireplace, the O'Rourkery, ca.
1902.

LETTER TO HER PARENTS

MAY 8, 1899 (AGE 32)

Wait till we live on the hill! Which translated means, won't we just have fun when Hill-Stead is a fact.

to be "an exact duplication of a farmhouse of eighty years ago."[9] While Clarence Cook had advocated for accent decoration with old American furniture, which he praised as rarely "ugly or awkward," Theodate's approach was more historical than aesthetic, more chaste than decorative.[10] As befitting her proximity to Hartford, which served as a center for collectors and scholars of American antiques during the last decade of the nineteenth century, she sought a more "authentic" look—one that offered a nostalgic retreat from the disorienting pressures of industrialization, urbanization, immigration, and economic fluctuations. In many ways her Colonial Revival tendency followed contemporary historic restoration practice and the taste of the Hartford circle. She turned to the Hartford architectural firm of Hapgood & Hapgood for additional renovations in 1892 and was friendly with such early Connecticut antiquarians as George Dudley Seymour.[11]

With her plan for a new house for her parents up the hill from the O'Rourkery, Theodate faced a new opportunity to develop a traditional decorative scheme within a building that drew heavily upon colonial American elements, including paneled wainscoting and Georgian fireplaces. As she wrote around 1920, "I designed and superintended the building of the house and it was my desire to have it furnished in keeping—that is in an old fashioned way."[12] Unlike Stanford White (1853–1906) and other influential New York tastemakers of the time, who often incorporated architectural elements from European homes as a form of interior decoration, Theodate created her own version of mid-eighteenth-century American Georgian architecture.[13]

While the architectural interior was conceived as a single, coherent piece by Theodate, the actual decorating scheme seems to have taken shape over time and with the involvement of all three Popes—Alfred, Ada, and Theodate. During the family's European travels, Alfred Pope often purchased not just paintings but also antique furniture and ceramics. On their European tour from fall 1888 to summer 1889, he purchased Chinese ceramics in Paris, Italian majolica in Venice and Paris, a mahogany clock and various small boxes in London, a marquetry table in Paris, and sundry antiques in Munich. While these items were acquired for the Cleveland house, most were brought to Farmington where they were integrated into the decorative scheme of the new home.[14]

In the spring of 1898, Theodate apparently picked out some furniture at Morrison's, a shop near Lord & Taylor in New York, but she did not actually oversee the entire process.[15] Instead Ada Pope seems to have been the coordinator of the decorative scheme, as is made evident in a letter from A. H. Davenport to McKim, Mead & White in the fall of 1900. Davenport, seeking access in order to copy the finish and an eagle finial of the "old cabinet" in the architectural firm's office, writes that the furniture firm was making a reproduction of a Federal-style breakfront for "Mrs. A. A. Pope."[16]

Rather than place the responsibility of decorating Hill-Stead in the hands of a commercial firm, all three Pope family members seem to have involved themselves in a cumulative process of acquiring furnishings over the decade preceeding the house's construction. In the spring of 1900, they all went shopping for furniture, carpets, and drapes in Baltimore, Philadelphia, New York, and Boston, purchasing antique furniture from small shops such as J. M. Wintrob Antiques in Philadelphia and H. C. Alley & Co. in Boston.[17] The final product bears evidence of each of the Popes' contribution.[18]

To gain a clear picture of Hill-Stead's original decorating scheme, it is necessary to knit together information from several different sources: photographs of the interior, published during the house's first decade in *The Architectcural Review* (1902), *The Architectural Record* (1906), and *American Homes and Gardens* (1910); the 1909 household inventory and the many surviving objects still in the house. As a result, this discussion necessarily centers on several of the main rooms depicted in the early photographs. In addition, because it has proved difficult to document many of the smaller art objects, as well as the dining wares, the focus of this essay is on floor and wall treatments, furniture and furniture arrangements, and the overall decorative philosophy.

The Hall, as befitting a Georgian center-hall plan, is a wide passageway that incorporated a stairway to the left (along the north wall) and opens up to the Georgian Parlor (as the 1909 inventory referred to the Living or Drawing Room) on the right (to the south). A wall-to-wall ingrain Wilton-style carpet covered the floor and stairs, its green and pink body and golden brown pattern complementing the deep tan or butterscotch color of the painted woodwork and the green patterns of the neoclassical wallpaper. For the carpeting, which also extended into the other public rooms on the first floor (the Drawing Room, Ell Sitting Room, and Dining Room), the Popes turned to the Whittall Rug Company in nearby Worcester, Massachusetts, even though they had purchased English carpets from a Boston importer on other

Entry Hall, *The Architectural Record*, August 1906

Upper Hall, *The Architectural Record*, August 1906

Entry Hall

occasions. Whittall, which relied upon English-style carpet looms, built up a national reputation at the end of the nineteenth century and satisfied the Popes' demanding standards for an eighteenth-century-style carpet.[19] Similarly, the wallpaper produced by M. H. Birge & Sons of Buffalo, New York, revived a type of large neoclassical pattern popular in the early national period and was very different from the William Morris–inspired papers of the Euclid Avenue house or the small-pattern papers of the O'Rourkery.[20]

The Popes relied upon antique mahogany furniture to set the tone for visitors who would enter the Hall through the front door. As throughout the house, historical furniture was more than an accent; it was the unifying principle. An American Empire sofa made between 1820 and 1840 was placed under the stairs and opposite a New England Federal-style card table flanked by a pair of Chippendale Revival chairs. A Scottish tall-case clock, three other Chippendale-style chairs, an English card table that closely resembled the work of New York cabinetmaker Duncan Phyfe, a looking glass made in the third quarter of the eighteenth century, and a late-nineteenth-century Irish-style pier table filled out the furnishings for this space. A series of framed prints—the work of artists ranging from Albrecht Dürer (1471–1528) to James McNeill Whistler (1834–1903)—hung along the stairway wall. In passing through the main door, the visitor would be faced with a view of the prints and stairway, the welcoming and tasteful furniture, and the open doorway to the Drawing Room, a link that was further reinforced through the continuation of the Whittall carpet and the butterscotch color of the wood paneling and trim.

The Drawing Room and the adjacent Ell Sitting Room continued the Georgian-style theme of the Entry Hall but these rooms had a very different decorative scheme. The wall treatment featured a "striped green Art Nouveau" paper, which picked up the green in the carpet, with a swag frieze above. Although the swag provided a neoclassical motif, the paper was not truly an historic one. Framing the windows were rose-colored satin damask curtains with a small medallion pattern in a tan color and cord-fringed box lambrequins. The green walls and rose fabric provided the overall tone to the room, but the principal visual element was the fireplace, located on the east wall.

As was true in each of the main public rooms on the first floor, the Popes used a work of art to establish both a focal point and a color scheme to be emphasized through other decorative arts. In the Drawing Room *Grainstacks, White Frost Effect* by Claude Monet (1840–1926) hung over the mantel, flanked by the artist's *Rock Points at Belle Ile* on the left and *Girl with Cat* by Pierre Auguste Renoir (1841–1919) on the right. The mantel decoration included two Abruzzi vases painted with mythological scenes, an Urbino bowl with a scene of a rocky coast that resonated with the *Belle Ile* painting, and two bronzes by Antoine-Louis Barye (1796–1875): one of a lioness and one of a horse. The blues, greens, and yellows in the Italian majolica garniture displayed just below *Grainstacks* brought out the same hues in the dabbed brushstrokes of the Impressionist painting and gave that end of the room a compelling visual focus. This effect was reinforced by a wide fireplace with black and yellow variegated marble facing and a black steel neoclassical grate, made for the room by William H. Jackson & Co. of New York.[21] Several other examples of Italian majolica with similar colors were displayed in an English mahogany cabinet on the northwest wall, as well as three large platters mounted on the wall, including a pair on either side of the bay window. To the left of the fireplace, the northeast corner of the room, hung Monet's *Fishing Boats at Sea*, the greens of which were accentuated by the wallpaper. On the opposite wall, above a piano, hung *The Guitar Player* by Edouard Manet (1832–1883), the yellows and greens of its parrot resonate with those of the majolica. Nearby, the rose of the ballerinas' tutus in *Dancers in Pink* by Edgar Degas (1834–1917) picked up similar tones in the upholstery fabric that covered much of the seating.

TOP: Drawing Room and Ell Sitting Room, *The Architectural Review*, November 1902

BOTTOM: Drawing Room and Ell Sitting Room, watercolor by Alfred Pope's nephew, Arthur Pope, ca. 1902

Functionally, the Drawing Room was furnished to display the paintings aesthetically, house the Steinway grand piano for enjoying musical performances, and for other social activities, and to provide an extensive number of forms of comfortable seating. In addition to several small tables and the cabinet containing majolica, the room included a large Empire-style center table supporting a neoclassical-style columnar lamp with a green silk damask shade. The table and lamp were located underneath a nineteenth-century chandelier that may have been removed from the Brooks' family house in Salem, Ohio.[22] Around this centrally located neoclassical core were spread seating in the mid-eighteenth-century Chippendale style, including three sofas, a love seat, eight armchairs, six side chairs, and several stools. Upholstered seating was given the highest priority, and period photographs demonstrate that side chairs filled the niches on either side of the fireplace, sofas lined the north and south walls, and armchairs and easy chairs inhabited the center of the room. Window seats with rose-colored cushions provided additional seating in the bay window area.[23]

The Ell Sitting Room was an extension of the Drawing Room and thus shared the same floor and wall treatments. In this more intimate space (the feel of which is created in part by its lower ceiling height), a smaller fireplace with variegated marble facing similar to that used in the Drawing Room was topped by a small mantel adorned with several pieces of pink lusterware ceramics.[24] Above the mantel hung the Monet painting *View of Cap d'Antibes*. The rose and green colors of this painting became highlighted in the room setting. A built-in cupboard housed equipment for various card games, suggesting a preferred use for this space. An antique gateleg table served as a gaming table, and six armchairs provided seating for card players. Additional seating for this room included a rocking chair, a wing chair, and a sofa flanked by a sewing table at each end. On the porch leading off the Ell Sitting Room, plank-seated Windsor settees and Colonial-style chairs with added rockers provided additional seating during warmer weather. Older Windsors, rush-seated turned chairs, or vernacular Chippendale-style chairs—all of them stripped of their original paint in accordance with the period collector's interest in clean surfaces that showcased the honest figure of the wood—were prevalent throughout Hill-Stead's various porches and contrasted with the dark gentility of the mahogany furniture used in the first-floor formal rooms.

The Dining Room could be entered through a door in the Ell Sitting Room or a door at the back of the Hall. These three rooms were further united by the pattern

Ell Sitting Room, *The Architectural Record*, August 1906

Dining Room, *American Homes & Gardens*, February 1910

of the Whittall carpet, although in the Dining Room the dominant color of the carpet shifts from pink to green with a touch of blue. In contrast to the painted woodwork of the Entry Hall and Ell Sitting Room, the woodwork of the Dining Room, including the built-in cabinet to the left of the fireplace and the boxed-in and paneled beams, featured faux graining painted to simulate oak, a wood valued by antiquarians for its associations with utility and strength.[25] Much of the furniture in the room provided the look of an early-nineteenth-century dining room. Ada Pope commissioned A. H. Davenport to make an antique-looking long, rectangular table capable of expanding to just over nineteen feet through the insertion of up to twelve leaves, to serve as the center of the furnishings. With this table, they assembled a set of twelve shield back chairs, several of which reveal extensive reworking to make them a set, and a New York–made Empire-style sideboard with urn-shaped knife boxes set on top.[26] Two Federal-style sofas provided additional seating along the south and northeast walls. The doored cupboard, based on mid-eighteenth-century examples, housed glassware. Additional antique accents included the Massachusetts Federal-period mantel clock, the mid-eighteenth-century tilt top tea table, and the Empire-style sofa table toward the north wall. Silver, displayed on the sideboard and on the shelved side tables to either side of it, ranged from French tea and coffee services by Odiot to antique English and Irish silver to contemporary Gorham flatware. Table runners for the main table were custom made of Asian silk to reinforce the color choices for the room.

The walls of the dining room were covered with a thick brown-colored cartridge paper patterned with small figures, and the window draperies were brown silk velour with shaded cream and brown trim and a boxed valance. Once again, the walls and floor provided an overall tone, and the real decorative emphasis was carried by the fireplace area and color achieved through paintings and ceramics. An elaborate brass insert with andiron pilasters and D-shaped apron and the pulvinated frieze make this the most decorative of the house's fireplaces. Above it hung Degas' pastel *Jockeys*, the soft greens of which provided the unifying element of the room. That green was picked up by the Chinese celadon vases on the mantel and by the dappled greens in Monet's *Grainstacks, in Bright Sun* directly across the room. The other colors in the Monet were drawn out by the other paintings flanking it along the west wall, including Manet's *Toreadors* to the south (toward the Ell Sitting Room) and Jacob Maris's (1838–1899) *View of Dordrecht with Cathedral* and Monet's *Oat and Poppy Field* to the north.[27] The Dutch mahogany china cabinet in the northwest corner of the

Jockeys, Edgar Degas (1886) hangs above the Dining Room fireplace mantel. The mantel, paneled wall, and all woodwork in this room are treated in a faux wood grain finish.

room, purchased from Duveen Brothers, displayed a colorful collection of English ceramics—green, copper, pink, and blue lusterware and a pale yellow Wedgwood service with white chrysanthemums—that also complemented the colors of the paintings along the west wall.[28]

A suite of rooms led off the north of the Entry Hall. Their distinction as more private was made obvious by the entry door, which swung open to conceal the door into the First Library, restricting easy visual and physical access. A change in carpeting also signified the shift into a different suite of rooms. In the Library was a reddish brown Whittall carpet with a light, gold lattice and rosette patterning. The faux oak graining of the paneling and the curtains of golden brown satin damask with bow knot and large floral medallion patterns reinforced the reddish brown tones of the room. Here, as in the other first-floor public rooms, pressed opalescent glass rosettes served as curtain tiebacks. Such glass accents paralleled the contemporary collecting interest in pressed glass cup plates made by the Boston and Sandwich Glass Company. While leather bound books lined three walls and bestowed a form of historical decoration, the east wall with the fireplace provided the decorative accents that established the distinctive character of this retreat. Within this golden glow, the red and black tortoiseshell mantel clock hung on the chimneybreast and the sang-de-boeuf Chinese ceramics on the mantel provided the deep red accents. Flanking the clock and above the ceramics were hung a series of mezzotints depicting prominent English writers, artists, and leaders, including Samuel Johnson, William Shakespeare, Laurence Sterne, Matthew Prior, Joshua Reynolds, William Pitt, Warren Hastings, and the Duke of Wellington. A late-seventeenth-century caned chair stood next to the well-articulated mantel, complete with dentil molding, and reinforced the theme of old England. Three other neoclassical-style chairs in the Library had cane foundations on which were laid cushions upholstered in the same brown damask used for the curtains. Other seating included an Empire-style sofa, a Hepplewhite-style settee, and an easy chair, all covered in the brown damask. Only a walnut table desk, with a fall front writing surface, broke up the monopoly of chairs, suggesting this was a room intended for reading and conversation more than writing.[29]

While the first-floor rooms have retained much of their original appearance, the bedrooms on the second floor have experienced more significant change, especially after Theodate married John Wallace Riddle (1864–1941) in 1916 and took over the two bedrooms on the south side of the house. Mrs. Pope, widowed since 1913, moved

Library, *American Homes & Gardens*, February 1910

First Library

Detail of red and black tortoiseshell
mantle clock in the Library

MAY 19, 1901 (AGE 34)

THE HOUSE BEGINS TO LOOK VERY SETTLED. ALL CARPETS DOWN AND FURNITURE IN PLACE. IT WILL NOT BE LONG NOW BEFORE WE ARE IN I HOPE. A MISS TALCOTT IS CATALOGUING AND PLACING THE BOOKS IN THE LIBRARY.

MAY 30, 1901

I AM WRITING IN THE NEW HOUSE AND SEE IT FOR THE FIRST TIME BY GASLIGHT. THIS ROOM AND THE DINING ROOM LOOK SO BEAUTIFUL TO ME IT IS HARD FOR ME TO SETTLE DOWN TO WRITING. MOTHER IS WORKING AWAY WITH HARRIET——I DO NOT KNOW WHAT ABOUT AND FATHER IS DOWN AT MY HOUSE TALKING ABOUT INSURANCE WITH YOUNG MR. WHITMORE.

LEFT: Opalescent pressed glass tiebacks in a petal and shell pattern at the Library windows. The same style tiebacks, in various sizes, are used at most of the windows throughout the house.

RIGHT: Ada Brooks Pope in the Ell Sitting Room, ca. 1910

to Theodate's former two-room suite. The Mulberry Suite, in the northwest corner, was one of the second-floor bedrooms that was photographed in the house's first decade and offers insights into the Popes' furnishing of a bedroom.[30] As was typical of most bedrooms in the late nineteenth century, the trim was painted in a light cream tone to frame the densely patterned wallpaper. In this bedroom, the early nineteenth-century-style paper featured flowers in a tight latticework. The rhythm of these flowers was also repeated in the carpet, which was a mulberry-colored Brussels with a small flower pattern. A larger and more flowing floral pattern, in mulberry and green, ornamented the art linen used for the window curtains and upholstery of the Davenport sofa, the easy chair at the foot of the bed, and the Shaker rocking chair.

Much of the furniture reinforced the early style of the wallpaper. The elaborately carved fourposter bed was newly made but resembled some of the beds carved by Samuel McIntire (1757–1811) and other craftsmen working in the early

Mulberry Suite, from *American Homes and Gardens*, February 1910

national period. A newly made dressing table with lyre supports evoked the New York Empire style made famous by Duncan Phyfe (1768–1854). Interspersed among these newer examples were antiques, including a bureau with bird's-eye maple panels on the drawer fronts, a Pembroke table, a corner basin stand, a work table, three white-painted fancy chairs with rush seats, and two Federal-period gilt looking glasses. The result is one of most time-specific decorative schemes in the house—one in which all the furniture dates from a similar period and provides the feeling of historical accuracy.

The mulberry color of the carpet was emphasized not only in the art linen but also by several tortoiseshell accessories and an extensive collection of ruby red Bohemian glass. The former included a mantel clock, several workboxes, and a toilet set; the latter consisted of a compote, a pair of candlesticks, a decanter and goblet, and several cologne bottles. No other room in the house had any such glass in spite of its great popularity in the nineteenth century and thus suggests a conscious concentration of it in this room. The artwork focused upon the theme of young girls and included two paintings by Mary Cassatt (1844–1926): *Sara Handing a Toy to the Baby* and *Antoinette Holding Her Child by Both Hands*, and a pastel by Berthe Morisot (1841–1895) of a young girl in a chair. Thus, in furnishing this room, the Popes wove together the themes of girlhood and early national America, and used the color red to provide the visual cohesion.

Although not illustrated in any early published photographs, Mr. and Mrs. Pope's bedroom, in the southeastern corner of the main house, revealed Mrs. Pope's interest in using color as a determining feature of the decoration. The 1909 inventory includes notes on colors, fabric types, patterns, and finishes used throughout the house. In this room, art linen rather than wallpaper covered the walls. A pattern of yellow trees set within a lattice pattern, also used for the curtains, complemented the yellowish tone of the woodwork grained in imitation of curly maple. Although there were several examples of dark mahogany furniture housed therein, this bedroom was distinguished by the high concentration of furniture made of lighter woods, which was unusual for formal or lived-in spaces. Mrs. Pope furnished her room with a maple Empire bureau with mahogany columns, a curly maple settee, a pair of pearwood chairs, a Pennsylvania mid-eighteenth-century curly maple lowboy with some additional carving, a New England curly maple highboy with a rebuilt lower section, a large satinwood worktable, and a stained maple Shaker rocker. The gathering of

The Mulberry Suite

An array of the Popes'
collection of ruby red
Bohemian glass

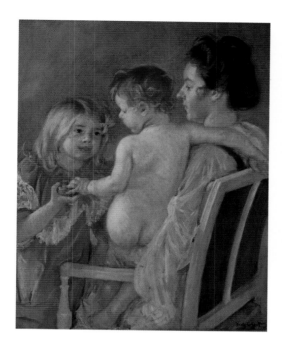 

such a high proportion of lighter wood furniture suggests more than coincidence. The yellowish tone of the Sienna marble mantel garniture set underscores this deliberate color scheme. The artwork in the Popes' bedroom consisted of a wide selection of Japanese woodblock prints. The coloration of the prints is predominantly greens and blues, a natural complement to the yellow tones and lighter woods used in this room.

Theodate's original two-room suite stood apart by reason of its historical rather than aesthetic emphasis, in spite of the white-enameled woodwork, wallpaper with pink rosebuds set within lattice, chintz curtains, and pink and white Brussels carpet. Within this more feminine setting sat some of the older antiques, including a simple fourposter bed, two Federal-era bureaus, an American maple drop leaf table, an American lolling chair, the base of a highboy, two slatback chairs, and an English worktable. More telling was the artwork on the wall: historical prints of such scenes as the Old Colony House in Newport, colonial churches in Providence, and a New England village street scene, as well as a Wallace Nutting photograph. The furnishing is more decidedly Colonial and Federal America, as it had been in the O'Rourkery. This suggests that Theodate asserted greater influence in her own rooms than

---

TOP LEFT: *Sara Handing a Toy to the Baby*, Mary Cassatt (ca. 1901), oil on canvas, 33" x 27"
TOP RIGHT: Ada Brooks Pope at her dressing table, ca. 1902. Photograph by Theodate Pope.

LEFT: Ada Brooks Pope's monogrammed bath towels RIGHT: Bathroom sink with marble counter and backsplash

throughout the other parts of the house, where she shared furnishing decisions with her parents.

The original furnishing of Hill-Stead thus seems to represent the culmination of all three Popes' endeavors, blending the interests of Mr. Pope in history and modern art, Mrs. Pope in color and suitability, and Theodate in the eighteenth and early nineteenth centuries. All three members of the family in essence served as decorators of the house, in which the mix of reproduction wallpapers and rugs, historic ceramics, Impressionist paintings, seventeenth- and eighteenth-century prints, and English and American antique furniture (some old, some heavily restored, and some completely new versions) provided the desired effect of patina, refinement, and artistic absorption. In many ways the path of the Popes resembles that of Charles Lang Freer (1854–1919), who responded to the ills of the modern urban and industrial environment not through the simple resurrection of the past but by pursuing knowledge of art history and developing a discriminating connoisseur's eye in pursuit of aesthetic spiritualism. The Popes' library included many books on world religions and mysticism, most acquired in the 1890 to 1910 period, as well as works by Bernard Berenson, Ralph Adams Cram, Henry Adams, and other so-called agnostic aesthetes who looked to art rather than religion as a source of deep spiritual comfort.[31]

Rather than a collection of authentic works gathered to make a historical statement, like a period room, Hill-Stead offers the look of the old as a point of contrast to the over-decorated Gilded Age work of the 1870s and 1880s, or to the Francophile interiors favored by New York elites at the turn of the century.[32] In many ways the genteel repose of Hill-Stead fulfilled Claude Bragdon's 1904 call for simplicity in composition, coherence and consistency in the ensemble, and individuality of expression in order to initiate the "fitness, unity, and beauty of an old Colonial parlor" in the contemporary home.[33] The Popes' philosophy anticipated the call by Elsie de Wolfe (1865–1960), the New York society decorator who became famous in the 1910s, for suitability, simplicity, and proportion in the decoration of houses. DeWolfe's concept of using color and also certain focal objects as organizing themes is also present, but mixed with a refined interest in loosely historic interiors in an Anglo-American style and in French art of the 1880s and 1890s.[34] The Popes' emphasis on the refined, artistic use of the past differs, however, from the subsequent interest in purer, more American interiors during the 1920s and 1930s—as evidenced by the opening of the American Wing at the Metropolitan Museum of Art in 1924

Mrs. Pope's suite, originally used as a guest room by daughter Theodate.

Theodate Pope's original
two-room suite

and of Colonial Williamsburg in 1929, the building of many small Colonial houses such as those by Royal Barry Wills, and the publication of books providing advice for historic furnishings by decorators such as Nancy McClelland (1877–1959).[35]

From the "house beautiful" of Clarence Cook to the simplified "good taste" of Elsie de Wolfe to the "American Georgian and Federal" rooms of Nancy McClelland, the Popes' interiors at Hill-Stead combined elements of all three furnishing philosophies. There is really only one other contemporary who shared their interest in collecting antiques and artworks and who responded to color and historical themes so directly. Henry Davis Sleeper (1878–1934) built and furnished the theatrical Beauport in Gloucester, Massachusetts, from 1907 to 1934.[36] Each of his rooms was organized around a different historical or literary theme (rather than a household function), creating specific compositions unified by color, material, or form. However, Sleeper's project was predominantly aesthetic. In contrast, the Popes seemed to pursue a cultural agenda. Their attention to refined taste in the materiality and historical association of household objects and the development of a coherent visual and haptic furnishing strategy parallels the importance of touch, empathy, and class consciousness in the writings of Henry James, who visited Hill-Stead in the early 1900s and wrote so eloquently about its effects.[37] The Popes' real claim was their ability to produce a stunning and comfortable interior, built upon history and color, that showcased their art in an intimate domestic setting.

At Hill-Stead, one can see Impressionist paintings as they were intended to be seen. This outstanding collection of masterpieces by the foremost painters of the movement has been preserved in the kind of domestic spaces for which Impressionism was originally designed. The high quality of Hill-Stead's collection, and the precise manner in which it is installed are an outgrowth of the natural talents and cultivated skills of two people: Alfred Atmore Pope (1842–1913), and his daughter, Theodate (1867–1946), respectively. Both operated in different contexts, which overlap at Hill-Stead: the history of Impressionism and the history of the collection museum.

The Collection

Alfred Pope had an extraordinary eye. He bought Impressionist paintings between about 1888 and 1907, while they were still very new and, to most people, frighteningly audacious. Yet he chose paintings whose quality has stood the test of time remarkably well. Stylistically, Impressionist paintings were characterized by dynamic tensions between inventively abbreviated handling of oil or pastel pigments and rigorously geometric compositions, as well as between three-dimensional illusion and two-dimensional surface design. The paintings Pope collected show these characteristics at their best, and with amazing consistency. Impressionism, however, was always about more than style. Impressionist paintings—especially those by James McNeill Whistler (1834–1903) in his French Impressionist phase, by Mary Cassatt (1844–1926), Gustave Caillebotte (1848–1894), Edgar Degas (1834–1917), Claude Monet (1840–1926), Berthe Morisot (1841–1895), Camille Pissarro (1830–1903),

The Tub, 1886, Edgar Degas, pastel on paper, 27 1/2" x 27 1/2"

and Pierre-Auguste Renoir (1841–1919), along with those by their friend and leader, Edouard Manet (1832–1883, who never officially became an Impressionist)—were simultaneously daring explorations of style and astute investigations into

TOP: View across the Drawing Room into the Ell Sitting Room with paintings by Monet, Degas, and Manet

BOTTOM: Drawing Room with works by Monet and Degas

the social issues experienced on a daily basis by the late-nineteenth-century Parisian middle class. Pope's collection includes such works by Cassatt, Degas, Monet, Manet, and Whistler, in addition to strong works by Eugène Carrière (1849–1906) and Pierre Puvis de Chavannes (1824–1898), somewhat conservative peers and friends of the Impressionists.

Consider for example the 1886 pastel Pope bought by Degas, *The Tub*. At once compellingly realistic and yet abstractly detached, the form of a woman's body is bent almost in two as she reaches down with her sponge to the shallow round tub in which she washes. The pose Degas has chosen for his model gives us, his audience, a sense of almost eerie intimacy with his image: we feel as if we are not just close to this woman in a very private moment but looking at her from an actual position in real space, right next to and above her. Ours is also a class and gender position: the scale and style of the room, the size and type of the tub, converge to identify her as a member of the comfortable working class in late-nineteenth-century Paris, which puts her in a relationship of inferiority to the artist Degas, a member of the very highest rank of the middle class. Meanwhile, the spatial relationship between the nude, bent model, tending to her cleanliness, and the artist, who works as he looks, also establishes the submission of her passive and bodily femininity to his critical and disembodied masculinity. Having created a simultaneously physical and psychological place for us in relation to his subject, Degas switches tactics and offers to our gaze a rippling cascade of peaches, violets, tans, and oranges, shot through with greens. The pastel marks barely blend into an illusion of three-dimensional form to produce a picture of a human back and arms. Instead, we're looking at an idea of how the interaction of light, color, and volume could be translated into pure color on a flat surface.

The Tub represents a socially explicit subject without being overtly political or historical. Pope was not attracted to the most controversial products of Impressionism. He did not buy scandalous paintings like Manet's 1863 *Olympia*, or even grimly modern visions of urban alienation like Caillebotte's 1877 *Place de l'Europe on a Rainy Day*. But Pope did not buy paintings that were merely pretty either; witness Degas's *The Tub*. His paintings by Cassatt, Degas, Manet, Monet, and Whistler are all outstanding examples of work by artists who have all remained at the heart of the Impressionist canon. When Henry James (1843–1916) described Hill-Stead in his 1904–05 travel essays on America, he used several metaphors to evoke the palatable yet powerful quality of Pope's paintings. He wrote that they

James McNeill Whistler in his studio, Paris, 1899

Portrait of the writer Henry James, 1910. Photograph by Theodate Pope.

treated us to the momentary effect of a large slippery sweet inserted, without warning, between the compressed lips of half-conscious inanition....no proof of the sovereign power of art could have been, for the moment, sharper....it was the sudden trill of a nightingale, lord of the hushed evening.[1]

Pope had reason to exclaim to Whistler, "[Y]ou know everything comes to the collector who waits. I believe I have the best—the finest—Degas and Manet in America and I want to overmatch them with the finest Whistler—we ought to bring this about—YOU and I—Well!"[2]

What made Pope form this exceptional collection of paintings? When he first started his Grand Tour of Europe, visiting the famous galleries and museums, he—like most people—found Impressionism to be too raw. By late 1888, however, his taste was rapidly changing, encouraged by his wife's brother, the artist Edward "Ned" M. Brooks (1853–1931), by Harris Whittemore (1864–1927), the son of a business associate and a discerning collector of Impressionism, and by the great dealer and promoter of Impressionism, Paul Durand-Ruel. Although in 1888 Impressionism, as a whole, had not been accepted outside a small circle of avant-garde thinkers, Monet had just made a commercial breakthrough, soon to be marked by his exhibition of grainstack paintings at the fashionable Petit Gallery in 1889—an exhibition that the Popes would see. Indeed, Pope bought two splendid examples of Monet's grainstack paintings from a third important gallery handling Impressionist work, Boussod & Valadon: *Grainstacks, White Frost Effect* and *Grainstacks, in Bright Sunlight*. By 1894,

Pope paid $12,000 for Manet's *The Guitar Player*, painted in 1866, a price so high it caused the Impressionist artist Camille Pissarro to call him a "nabob."[3] A combination of his natural taste for strong, innovative quality and his ability to recognize good advice had put him, not in advance of the market curve, but at its leading edge.

From the prints Pope collected to complement his paintings it is clear that he fully understood the visual climate of Impressionism. He acquired a number of Japanese Ukiyo-e prints. Ukiyo-e prints began to be imported into France almost as soon as Japanese ports were opened to American and European commerce in 1853, and they had rapidly begun to exert a deep formal influence on the circle of artists committed to the representation of modern life, some of whom became the Impressionists. Among the Impressionists, Cassatt, Degas, and Morisot all owned Japanese prints; Monet collected so many he could cover almost all the walls of his country house at Giverny with them. Pope concentrated his Ukiyo-e purchases on the same artists the Impressionists valued most highly, notably Katsushika Hokusai (1760–1849), Suzuki Harunobu (1724–1770), Kitagawa Utamaro (1750–1806), and Ando Hiroshige (1797–1858).

Meanwhile, Pope also bought the same sorts of European prints admired by those who promoted Ukiyo-e. Appreciation of Japanese prints was one element in an 1860s print revival. Turning away from the lithographic technique that had swept the print world in the first half of the century, engravers, such as Jules Jacquemart (1837–1880) and Félix Braquemond (1833–1914), renewed artistic interest in both contemporary etchings and engravings by artists like Charles Méryon (1821–1868) and older engravings by artists like Albrecht Dürer (1471–1528) and Giovanni Batista Piranesi (1720–1778). The Hill-Stead print collection includes work by Félix Bracquemond, Méryon, Dürer, and Piranesi, as well as several prints by Whistler, the American who carried the print revival forward in the 1880s.

Pope's letters reveal that he relished meeting personally the creators of the paintings he bought and that he valued their character. In a letter written on August 25, 1894, he described with pleasure a visit with Monet at Giverny, its garden "large and beautifully cultivated as *the wonderful amount and variety* of flowers testified:"

> *Monet strikes you as sturdy & strong in physique and intellect—a fine soft-brown*
> *eye—one that sees everything—A lovely smile—a clever man—you wouldn't take him*
> *for an artist—more like a business man turned from town to country.*[4]

The Guitar Player,
Edouard Manet (1866),
oil on canvas,
25" x 31 1/2"

*Grainstacks, White
Frost Effect,* Claude
Monet (1889), oil on
canvas, 25 1/4" x 36"

*Grainstacks, in Bright
Sunlight,* Claude
Monet (1890), oil on
canvas, 23" x 38"

The 53 Stations of the Tokaido, Rain at Shono, Ando Hiroshige (1833), woodblock print, 10 1/2" x 15 1/2"

The 53 Stations of the Tokaido, Nissaka, Ando Hiroshige (1833–34), woodblock print, 11 1/4" x 16 3/4"

One of 36 Views of Mt. Fuji, Inume Pass in Kai Provence, 1831, Katushika Hokusai, woodblock print, 11 3/4" x 16 3/4"

Pope appreciated Monet's business sense and liked to know he was paying good money for good work: "M said he has spent 3 years over these pictures & was going to have 15000 frs for them (~$3000) that he wouldn't be paid less for his time at less price…I would like two of them."[5] Pope felt a visceral dislike for painters who, though extremely popular, were also staunchly academic. "Masters like Gerome and Cabanel are turning out *wretched stuff* in their old age."[6] He had contempt for those "people who buy *on a name*" rather than because of a painting's quality.[7] He himself felt he had to "rise to" or feel an emotional and intellectual connection to a painting in order to want it.[8]

More broadly, Pope was self-educated and had earned his fortune in manufacturing iron parts for vehicles, notably as president of the National Malleable Castings Company. He was, therefore, part of that late-nineteenth-century American business class whose capitalist, democratic, individualist values were perfectly expressed by Impressionism. When the Impressionists first organized the exhibitions that gave them their name and forged their reputations in 1874, for instance, they literally constituted themselves as a corporation, complete with shares and in the hopes of profit. It is all too often forgotten that while the initial critical reaction to the style of paintings in the early Impressionist exhibitions was very mixed, the response to the entrepreneurial, private-sector capitalism of the exhibitions was uniformly positive. More profoundly, Impressionism fostered the values of individualism through both the behavior of its members and the work they created, even when those values were difficult to accept or understand.

RIGHT: *Old Battersea Bridge*, James McNeill Whistler (ca. 1879), etching, 9 1/2" x 13 1/4"
LEFT: *The Gleaners*, Jean-François Millet (ca. 1855–56), etching, 12" x 15 1/2"

MAY 9, 1889 (AGE 22)

TODAY WE SPENT ALL THE TIME FROM HALF
PAST TEN IN THE MORNING UNTIL FIVE IN THE
AFTERNOON AT THE EXPOSITION....NOW THE
IMPRESSIONISTS ARE INTERESTING, BUT I DOUBT
IF ANY OF THE WORK THEY ARE NOW DOING WILL
LAST. IT HAS ITS PLACE IN THE HISTORY OF ART
BECAUSE THEY CAME IN JUST THE RIGHT TIME.
THEY ARE SHOWING US THAT NATURE SHOULD BE
STUDIED OUT OF DOORS & THAT NO LANDSCAPE
OUGHT TO BE PAINTED IN THE STUDIO. THEY
ARE BRINGING US A FRESHNESS THAT COROT,
ROUSSEAU, DAUBIGNY AND THE OTHER ARTISTS OF
THAT SCHOOL NEVER DREAMED OF. NEVER THE
LESS THEY ARE GOING TOO FAR IN THE OPPOSITE
DIRECTION BUT STILL IT TAKES SOME MEN TO GO
BEYOND THE LINE IN ORDER TO BRING OTHERS
TO IT OR AS PAPA SAYS THE IMPRESSIONISTS ARE
SHOUTING IN ORDER TO BE HEARD. THE WISEMEN
WILL FOLLOW THEM ONLY THEY WILL GO SLOWLY
AND NEVER GO QUITE AS FAR.

Mary Cassatt was a guest at Hill-Stead. Her painting *Sara Handing a Toy to the Baby* (ca. 1901), 33" x 27", hangs in a second-floor guest bedroom.

Take Pope's acquisition of Cassatt's *Sara Handing a Toy to the Baby* of about 1901, for example. The very fact that Pope was willing to collect paintings by a woman reflects Impressionism's willingness to include a woman among its core members, with no questions asked, not to mention the openness of an Old World French group of colleagues to embrace a New World American. In the Hill-Stead painting, as in Cassatt's many others on the same subject, the artist celebrates the mother-child relationship as the basis of the modern, nuclear, secular family. In doing so, she abandoned centuries of Catholic theological meanings attached to what continued to be called the subject of "the Madonna." Cassatt, moreover, was unique among the painters of modern life in her renderings of the sensual pleasures of motherhood, which brought into the history of art a new and feminine perspective. Cassatt's fully dressed mother enjoys the embrace of her naked baby, bonded to it not merely by the idea of the mother-child relationship but by Cassatt's choice of unified color and composition. Passing along her experience from one generation of women to another, the mother in Cassatt's painting initiates her daughter into the pleasures of maternity, showing her infant to the little girl within the image, just as Cassatt shows the infant to us, her viewers.

Charles Baudelaire (1821–1867) in his paradigmatic book *The Painter of Modern Life* of 1863 never imagined such a modern life experience as Cassatt represented. His view of modernity was decidedly masculine and public. So was the view of the two great early French collectors of Impressionism, Gustave Caillebotte (1848–1894) and Isaac de Camondo (1851–1911). Both men formed their collections with the intention of donating them to the French state in order to force the rapid acceptance of Impressionism into national museums and into the history of French art. Neither of them included works by either Mary Cassatt or Berthe Morisot, though of course Caillebotte (himself a painter) knew his two female colleagues and their work very well. Pope, obviously, had a different view of Impressionism's modernity, which made his collection more daring in this respect than those of his French peers. Three factors might explain his choice: his nationality, the domestic destination of the collection, and the influence of his daughter, Theodate.

Unlike the Caillebotte and Camondo collections, the great early private American collections that form the nucleus of New York's Metropolitan Museum of Art and the Art Institute of Chicago collections of Impressionist paintings did include paintings by Cassatt. This may have had something to do with the fact that they were formed by women: Louisine Havemeyer and Bertha Honore Palmer, respectively. It may also have had something to do with Havemeyer's long, close friendship with Cassatt, and Palmer's meeting with Cassatt in 1889, which led her to commission a monumental mural from Cassatt for the pioneering Woman's Building at the 1893 World's Columbian Exposition in Chicago. Patriotism, too, certainly played a part. It was satisfying to realize that a fellow American had achieved such prominence in the French artistic avant-garde; and for Americans art-shopping in Paris, Cassatt's nationality could have outweighed her gender when it came to winning their trust. Nor was Cassatt shy about advising the purchase of her own work.[9] Nonetheless, Havemeyer's and Palmer's willingness, among that of other American collectors, to take Cassatt's advice on the purchase of paintings is part of a broader American tendency to accept the femininity of Impressionism, which contrasts with French collecting tendencies.

As for Pope, he also could have been thinking in advance of hanging his paintings in a home. He would not have been alone, even among French collectors. Though the Caillebotte and Camondo collections ultimately had public purposes, most collectors of Impressionism were furnishing middle-class homes. Whether they lived in city apartments or in country houses, Impressionism's patrons were overwhelmingly upper middle class: people very much like the Impressionist artists themselves. It is a myth that the Impressionists struggled, unrecognized, in poverty during their youth. They always had friends and patrons, who bought their paintings because they admired their beauty and also because they saw themselves and their lives reflected in them. And then they hung the paintings in their homes, where the works looked like they belonged.[10]

In their scale and color, as well as in their subjects, Impressionist paintings made in the 1860s, 1870s, and 1880s were conceived of in terms of middle- or upper-middle-class domestic spaces. Only the rare work, such as Caillebotte's *Place de l'Europe*, was so big that it required an institutional space in which to hang. Later, art historians would chide Impressionism for this very modesty of scale, arguing that only Manet's early, large-scale work could claim a place in the great European tradition of masterpiece paintings. The extremely influential early-twentieth-century English critic Roger Fry, for instance, accused Impressionism of having a "deplorable" influence on Manet's ambitions, which he contrasted with Cézanne's determination to produce "Museum pictures."[11] Note that the Manet painting Pope paid so much for, *The Guitar Player*, measured only 25 by 31½ inches.

Seen above a hearth, hung on a strongly patterned wallpaper, near window and ceiling moldings, mirrors, ornamental textiles, and densely arranged carved

View of Cap d'Antibes
(1888), Claude Monet,
oil on canvas,
25 3/4" x 31 3/4"

wood furniture, a painting like Monet's *View of Cap d'Antibes* (1889) needs its intense, shimmering pinks and blues to stand within its domestic setting. The color palettes of most Impressionist paintings add a chromatic focal point to the interior decoration styles of late-nineteenth-century Europe and North America, as well as to the conservative styles of the early twentieth century, such as Hill-Stead's neo-colonialism. Perhaps needless to say, this was especially true when the paintings were modestly framed by the Impressionists themselves, who sometimes experimented with straight painted frames, rather than in the overly ornate and gilded examples that weigh down so many Impressionist paintings in many museums today.[12]

And surely, the unusual inclusion of the women Impressionists in the Pope collection must owe something to the unusual personality of Theodate Pope. From her earliest days, Theodate displayed a sense of self rare among women of her time; and she acted with rare determination to expand her opportunities. In 1886, at the age of nineteen, she observed in her diary, "But how many girls are anxious to excel in a given thing and perhaps only one of a thousand succeeds."[13] That same year, she began to change her life by changing her name: from the one her parents had given her, Effie, to one rather grander, which she had chosen for herself—that of her paternal grandmother, Theodate. The next year she confided to her diary, "When will I find my

View of Cap d'Antibes, the first Impressionist painting Alfred Pope purchased, hangs above the Drawing Room mantel paired with Italian majolica.

ON BUYING MONET'S *VIEW OF CAP D'ANTIBES*

MAY 11, 1889 (AGE 22)

WENT UP TO GOUPILS AND MET UNCLE
NED AND MAMA THERE AFTER THEY
HAD FINISHED SHOPPING FOR AUNT
ALICE. PAPA BOUGHT A CLAUDE MONET
AND ANOTHER CARRIERE; A PORTRAIT
OF A BABY. DID NOT LIKE THE MONET AT
FIRST BUT NOW I THINK IT IS THE FINEST
IMPRESSION I HAVE YET SEEN. WE COULD
NOT APPRECIATE IT HAD WE NOT BEEN
IN THE MIDI.

ON FIRST SEEING *HAYSTACKS*

AUGUST 16, 1889 (AGE 22)

WE ALL, COUNTING UNCLE NED, WERE AT
PETIT'S GALLERY THIS MORNING TO SEE
AN EXHIBITION OF MONET'S. BEST IN THE
COLLECTION WAS A PICTURE OF HAY COCKS
IN THE EARLY MORNING WITH THE SUN
SHINING ON THE FROST THAT COVERED
THEM.

AUGUST 19, 1889

WE WENT TO GOUPIL TO SEE IF WE CAN GET
GELE BLANCHE; THAT FINE ONE, BY MONET.
I DOUBT IF THE MAN WHO OWNS IT WILL
SELL IT THIS SOON.

Grainstacks, White Frost Effect,
Claude Monet (1889) hangs in
the Drawing Room.

A detail of *Grainstacks, White Frost Effect* with its brilliant oranges, greens, and violets

vocation? Have I one?"[14] She declined an offer of marriage from Harris Whittemore in order to find a vocation of her own. In 1890, Theodate decided to settle in Farmington, Connecticut, where she had attended Miss Porter's School. Afterwards, she persuaded her parents to move and build a house there. Very exceptionally, in 1914, as a single woman, she took in a two-year-old foster child, Gordon Brockway, whose death from polio in 1916 devastated her.

Theodate accompanied her parents on their collecting trips. Like her parents, she did not at first embrace Impressionism wholeheartedly, though by August 1889 she had not only become an enthusiast but described that enthusiasm as something she and her father shared.[15] After embracing Impressionism, however, she sparred with one of its leading proponents on the value of art in society. Theodate and her parents met Mary Cassatt initially in 1898, while the painter was in the United States. Then, during the first years of the 1900s, the Popes saw Cassatt again and met the painter's great friend Louisine Havemeyer. Theodate spent much of 1903 in Paris and saw Cassatt frequently that year. Cassatt's correspondence with Havemeyer reveals that Theodate had decidedly different opinions about the value of art than her peers. She had the temerity to tell Cassatt that paintings were "a bore," and so were collections of paintings. Cassatt wrote to Havemeyer, "[Theodate] wants to know if your collection is not to be thrown open to the Public? She believes all pictures should be in public galleries!...I am afraid she will never give her parents much happiness," Cassatt lamented.[16]

Both Alfred Pope and his daughter sold works from the collection. Alfred had a fluid approach to his collecting, often selling works back to dealers or trading them for credit on the purchase of others, but always striving to own the best and desiring works that resonated with him emotionally. Theodate, on the other hand, sold works from the collection for a specific reason—funding the construction and operations of Avon Old Farms School, in nearby Avon, Connecticut, which she built as a memorial to her parents. In spite of her abundant resources, she found it necessary to sell a few paintings. She did so, however, with an eye toward remaining true to her father's collecting aims and leaving behind a legacy that accurately reflected his vision.

The Installation

"Rooms must be pictures," Theodate Pope had declared in 1911, according to Mary Cassatt.[17] Theodate had decided she wanted to become an architect, someone for whom rooms, rather than paintings would be the medium of choice. And Theodate did indeed become an architect, getting her real start by designing Hill-Stead for her parents. Two aspects of the Hill-Stead design story need to be taken into account when assessing her architectural achievements: Theodate's strategy of using the domesticity of Hill-Stead as a screen for her professional ambitions, and the role the installation of her father's painting collection played in those ambitions.

When, in 1898, on behalf of her father, Theodate approached the eminent firm of McKim, Mead & White about designing the house, she knew the firm's interest in taking on the project would be enhanced by the reputation her father's collection had already gained. She needed the firm to be very interested, because she had a plan they might resist. The firm did respond positively. Then Theodate sprang her trap. She wrote a letter to William Rutherford Mead explaining her intention to design the house herself, leaving only the working drawings and supervision of construction to the firm. Considering that she—a young, single woman—was a complete amateur, and he was one of the most prominent architects in the country, her tone was astonishingly peremptory:

TOP: *Jockeys* (1886), Edgar Degas, pastel on paper, 15 1/4" x 34 3/4"

RIGHT: View through Entry Hall into Dining Room with *Jockeys*

[A]s it is my plan, I expect to decide in all the details as well as all more important questions of plan that may arise. This must be clearly understood at the outset, so as to save unnecessary friction in the future. In other words, it will be a Pope house instead of a McKim, Mead, and White.[18]

As it turned out, Theodate proved willing to let the firm take official credit for the house. In November 1902, notably, *The Architectural Review* ran a feature on the "House of Alfred A. Pope Esq." and attributed it to "McKim, Mead & White, Architects."[19] What Theodate got in exchange was a substantial reduction in the firm's usual fees and the more valuable recognition of her contribution to the house. She parlayed her experience with the firm into the facsimile of an apprenticeship—one convincing enough to enable her to become one of the first licensed women architects in America, with a long and productive career.[20]

While the authorship of Hill-Stead's architecture might have been ambiguous at the time, everyone recognized Theodate's work on its interior decoration. In February 1910, for instance, architectural historian Barr Ferree reported on "the zealous assistance of Miss Pope, to whom much of the interior treatment is due" in his article for *American Homes and Gardens*. "The paintings on the walls," he continued, "are, of course, modern, and are a part of the collection of masterpieces accumulated by the owner of this beautiful house."[21] Prominently displayed also were the Popes'

LEFT: Mary Cassatt in her home in France, ca. 1903. Photograph by Theodate Pope. RIGHT: Drawing Room with paintings by Monet and Renoir, *The Architectural Record*, August 1906

prints, both Japanese and European. Describing Hill-Stead in John La Farge and August Jacacci's landmark 1907 guide to the greatest private American art collections, Kenyon Cox emphasized the effect of its overall installation:

> *There is no museum-like crowding of beautiful things, yet beautiful things are everywhere: a few good pieces of old china here and there, Japanese prints, a Dürer engraving or two, etchings by Méryon and Haden and Whistler, and some thirty paintings of the most modern schools, choice works, selected with a fine discrimination and hanging well apart with a luxury of space that emphasizes their individual beauty.... [T]he general effect is of coolness and freshness and light, the paintings harmonizing admirably with the airy brightness of such a country house.*[22]

When in 1911 Theodate pronounced to Cassatt that "rooms must be pictures," she had already, in fact, designed rooms around pictures. Like many European and North American women in the second half of the nineteenth century, Theodate had availed herself of the femininity attributed to domesticity in general and to interior decoration in particular. She was among a significant number of women who concealed the extent of their public ambitions by hiding behind an art collection that pretended to furnish a home. There were women like Louisine Havemeyer and Bertha Palmer who built collections and installed them in their homes, and then gave them away. There were several American women who founded major museums, only to efface themselves soon after: women like Abigail Aldrich Rockefeller, Lillie P. Bliss, and Mrs. Cornelius J. Sullivan, who began the Museum of Modern Art in the late 1920s (inaugurated 1929); Gertrude Vanderbilt Whitney, who began the Whitney Museum of American Art, also in the late 1920s (inaugurated 1931); and Hilla Rebay, who brought into being the New York Guggenheim Museum by 1937. And then there were women who built collections and installed them in their homes in order to eventually found public institutions and leave their personal mark forever in the public domain of art.

All across Europe and the United States, between about 1870 and 1940, women founded or cofounded museums that preserved their art collections just as they had installed them. The first woman to cofound a collection museum was Josephine Bowes, who together with her husband instituted the Bowes Collection in Barnard, England, in 1869. The most famous woman among the museum founders is probably Isabella Stewart Gardner, who boldly named a museum in Boston, Massachusetts,

entirely after herself—a museum that Theodate Pope certainly knew. In Europe, the Hallwylska Museet in Stockholm was founded by Wilhelmina van Hallwyll around her collection, as was the Kröller-Müller Museum in Oterloo, Holland, by Helene Kröller-Müller. Following Peggy Guggenheim's death in 1979, the Venice Guggenheim Museum was founded in 1980 with her private collection. The Musée Jacquemart-André in Paris was founded and installed by Nélie Jacquemart around a collection she had assembled with her husband. The Musée Mayer van den Bergh in Antwerp was installed and founded by Henriette Mayer van den Bergh around both a main collection assembled by her son and a smaller collection amassed on her own. The objects in the Wallace Collection in London were assembled by successive generations of men, but it was a woman, Amélie Wallace, who donated the collection to the British nation. In the United States, the Wheelwright Museum in Santa Fe, the Hyde Collection in Glens Falls, New York, and Dumbarton Oaks in Washington, D.C., were founded by women: Mary Cabot Wheelwright, Charlotte Pruyn Hyde, and Mildred Bliss, respectively. The Ringling Museum in Sarasota, Florida, was the joint work of John and Mable Ringling. The Huntington Art Gallery, founded by a man, was instigated behind the scenes by a woman—Arabella Huntington.

View through First Library into Second Library with *The Blue Wave, Biarritz* (1862), James McNeill Whistler, oil on canvas, 25 3/4" 35"

"All pictures should be in public galleries!" Theodate Pope insisted to Cassatt in 1903.[23] Like the other collection museums founded by both women and men, Hill-Stead looked like a home—and functioned as such for years—but was destined to become a public gallery. In the case of Hill-Stead, the lag between the design of a home and the inauguration of a museum was especially long, protracted over forty-five years and two generations of owners. Nonetheless, the idea that Hill-Stead would become a museum took hold early in its history, as Theodate's pronouncement indicates. At least in Theodate's mind, the intention to found a museum was germinating long before Hill-Stead ceased being used as a house by her parents, and long before she began to live there with her husband, John Riddle, in 1916. Theodate inherited Hill-Stead when her mother died in 1920 and she left the house to the public at her own death in 1946. By stipulation in her will, nothing in the house is to be moved, lent, or sold.

So if places like Hill-Stead were intended to become museums, why were they installed to look like homes? In an era that closely associated the home with individuality, leaving behind a fossilized house was like leaving behind an imprint of the self. To memorialize oneself (or, as Theodate Pope said in her will, one's parents) was perfectly compatible with the notion of public philanthropy, because this was also an era that believed in the value of an intimate experience of art as an alternative to the numbing vastness of municipal or national museums. A visit to a collection museum promised the opportunity to feel at home with art, as well as with the memory of the founder.

The public value of the collection museum seemed all the more compelling because the idea of a home offered an easy pretext for the installation of high art among works of decorative art and even ordinary furnishings. Traditional art museums adopted an increasingly rigorous organization of artworks by medium, geography, and chronology, whereas the collection museum displayed complete environments in which art objects seemed "at home" and therefore somehow alive. Of course, both sorts of museums applied classifying systems. The classifying systems of traditional museums were merely more obviously artificial, whereas the signs of domesticity invoked by collection museums appeared much more natural. Although private domestic spaces as we still know them were invented during the seventeenth and eighteenth centuries, by the second half of the nineteenth century they were completely taken for granted by the audiences of collection museums. Despite the presence of any number of great works of art, and despite the rational awareness that a place was a public museum, museum visitors would instantly—instinctively, it was believed—identify spaces as living rooms, dining rooms, studies, parlors, boudoirs, and bedrooms based on combinations of spatial scale and furniture choices.

Most importantly, the collectors who turned their possessions into museums believed that their installations were their personal creations. A good collection is always more than the sum of its parts. Whatever criteria used by collectors to acquire, their collecting habits emphasize some aspects of objects rather than others. Alfred Pope's criteria, for instance, helped make Impressionism prominent among all contemporary paintings: within that sphere, his choices reinforced the quiet order and chromatic complexity of Impressionism. A collector who devotes thought and care to the installation of his or her collection adds a whole new layer of meaning to it, which alters or compounds the meanings already gathered around separate objects. In the case of Hill-Stead, the difference between selection and installation is unusually evident, because each was the work of a different person.

The men and the women who turned their collections into museums used their wills not only to stipulate the preservation of their installations but also to express their sense of authorship. The women's wills expressed a special urgency because women were barred from so many other forms of artistic expression. In her 1912 will, Nélie Jacquemart explained,

> *These collections and their arrangement have been the goal of my studies, and my work has put its mark on them; my intention and my wishes are absolutely that no object be moved. Their ensemble and their harmony to which my taste is attached are to be respected—I hope that they will serve the studies of those who are devoted to art and its history.*[24]

Leaving a legacy affirming women's right to education, Wilhelmina van Hallwyl decreed in her will that the curator of her museum must always be a woman with a doctorate.

In her will, Theodate Pope made the same move, but more successfully. Of all the women museum founders, it was Theodate who most powerfully used the installation of a collection to escape the constraints of gender and start a career for herself, and who knew by the time she wrote her will how much she had accomplished.

Her father's collection had been the bait she had used to lure McKim, Mead & White, and she kept the collection at the heart of the house whose integrity her will ordained in perpetuity. When she turned Hill-Stead into a public institution, she was turning into a museum not only her father's collection but also the work with which she had made her crucial transition from amateur to professional architect.

Ironically, Theodate Pope's will contains one of the most ambivalent phrases among all the wills that found collection museums. "People should not be allowed to visit the museum too often, or stay too long, particularly if they annoy others."[25] What was she thinking? We do not know for sure, but nineteenth-century women often felt obliged to disclaim the public reach of their ambitions. Pay no attention. Come often and stay a long time. The beautiful collection and historic installation of Hill-Stead deserve every minute.

View of *Dancers in Pink* (ca. 1876), Edgar Degas, oil on canvas, 23 1/4" x 29 1/4" in Drawing Room

THE LANDSCAPE, GARDENS, AND FARM *Allyson M. Hayward*

As a schoolgirl, Theodate Pope (1867–1946) often wrote about someday having a farm. Her frequent musings came to fruition when the estate that came to be called Hill-Stead, was built on a verdant hillside overlooking the gently sloping farmlands in Farmington, Connecticut. Over the course of twenty years, Theodate, together with her parents, Alfred Atmore Pope (1842–1913) and Ada Brooks Pope (1844–1920), carefully planned and oversaw construction of a 250-acre experimental and working farm, which would eventually contain ornamental and vegetable gardens, orchards, greenhouses, a summer house, stone walls, and barns complete with livestock—all the trappings of its flourishing Colonial Revival predecessor. In keeping with their place in society, and with Alfred Pope's interest in competitive sport, a tennis court and golf "grounds" rounded out the picture.

Although the property took shape from the multifaceted interests of the entire Pope family, the design of the estate primarily reflects the work of Theodate Pope. Stylistically, Hill-Stead's landscape reflects the influence of various design traditions, including the English landscape movement, the Colonial Revival, and the Arts and Crafts movement. During its planning stages it also benefitted from Theodate's consultation with Warren H. Manning (1860–1938), a pioneer in the nascent field of landscape architecture, and later from Beatrix Farrand (1872–1959), a founding member of the American Society of Landscape Architects.

Located east of the Farmington River and directly adjacent to the village of Farmington, Hill-Stead lies within hills surrounding a fertile floodplain. Theodate possessed a great interest in agriculture and scientific farming. She envisioned a landscape that resembled a traditional New England farm. Yet it was also to be developed as a country place, which accommodated the leisure pursuits of its owners while providing domestic comfort and aesthetic qualities of elegance and refinement.

Aerial view of Hill-Stead, with farm complex in the foreground and house and carriage barn in the background

Inspired by the eighteenth-century *ferme ornée*,[1] or ornamental farm, of the English gentry, Hill-Stead is one of dozens of similar properties that sprang up all over New England in the late-nineteenth and early-twentieth centuries. Its design reflected a pastoral parkland with serpentine walks and avenues, special plantings, and framed vistas. Situated within this framework of Arcadian splendor, was a working farm.

The layout of Hill-Stead was influenced by the principles fostered by contemporary agricultural associations. It extended an earlier wave of agricultural experimentation, which included cattle and sheep breeding, and combined the utilitarian with the ornamental. Societies for the advancement of agriculture in America were originally established in 1785 in South Carolina and Pennsylvania. During the decade that followed, such societies spread rapidly throughout New England and, fifty years later, dominated the farming scene. These associations helped establish a belief in the scientific basis of agriculture, and progressive owners of country estates, such as the Popes, sought to integrate scientific practices into their farming operations. Hill-Stead and estates like it served as emblems of progressive social ideals for the upper class, as they provided a means by which their wealthy and privileged owners could give something back to society and to those less fortunate than themselves.[2]

The Popes ran the farm not as a profit-making enterprise (although they kept tight control over the farm's finances) but as a place to develop and maintain modern, sanitary conditions. Their research tested many theories of crop propagation and of livestock management and production that the average small farmer could not afford to undertake.[3] The knowledge gathered from these practices was subsequently shared with the larger community through published articles.

Although all three members of the Pope family shaped the development of Hill-Stead, Theodate's influence was the strongest. Letters in the Hill-Stead archives indicate that the idea of a farm similar to Hill-Stead loomed large in Theodate's childhood fantasies. She recorded these dreams frequently in her diaries. In one of her schoolgirl journals dating from 1887 she declared, "I look forward to a life on a farm with the little children I shall adopt."[4] Ten years later, Theodate persuaded her parents to build a home in rural Farmington to fulfill at least a part of that dream. Having boarded at Miss Porter's School in Farmington, she knew the area well and had many happy memories of residing there.

TOP: Hill-Stead farm and dairy, ca. 1902

RIGHT: Hill-Stead farm, including Hay and Horse Barns, Shepherd's Cottage, and eighteenth-century Farm House

Theodate's avid interest in developing a farm may have been influenced by a number of factors. Ada Pope's family had long operated a farm in Vermont. Always fascinated with New England's past, Theodate grew especially keen on the colonial period at about the same time the Colonial Revival movement swept the country as a whole. Her enthusiasm for colonial history shaped her lifestyle and her choices while building Hill-Stead. She was inspired by George Washington's home at Mount Vernon, Thomas Jefferson's at Monticello, and James Madison's at Montpelier, likely associating (as was the custom of the period) these cultivated landscapes with what she had read of their owners' high ideals and commitment to social good.[5] Like these founding fathers, Theodate chose the *ferme ornée* as the prototype for developing her property. By blending ornamental elements with features of a working farm and by emphasizing utility, horticultural variety, and pastoral openness throughout, this model served as an expression of an ideal social order

The transformation of various parcels of farmland into a country estate at Hill-Stead was based not only on the period's nostalgic look back at its colonial past but also on another nationally pervasive influence—the Arts and Crafts movement. Rapidly spreading across Britain, Canada, and the United States, and at its height from 1890 to 1910 (just as the Popes were developing Hill-Stead), the movement rejected the dehumanizing effects of industrial production and stressed simplicity, utility, and craft. It romanticized personal handiwork and encouraged the highest possible quality of workmanship and design. The revival of local traditions and the reuse of materials found on the land were commonplace aspects of this movement in landscape design: for example, stone cleared from the fields found its way into walls and bridges, and wooden poles made from felled trees were laced together to form pergolas for roses and vines. Theodate was intrigued by the Arts and Crafts movement; its emphasis on the domestic and vernacular landscape perfectly complemented her interest in living a rural lifestyle.[6]

From her exposure to the beauty of eighteenth-century English landscape parks sprang Theodate's appreciation for a unified landscape.[7] The Popes assembled the bulk of Hill-Stead's 250-acre farmstead between 1898 and 1901 through the systematic purchase of smaller properties. These included working farms, wood lots, and even an existing orchard.[8] The rolling pastures, hills, meadows, woodlands, swampy lowlands, and stream lent themselves well to treatment in the English park aesthetic Theodate had seen on her trips abroad.

Letters in the Hill-Stead archives indicate that Alfred Pope encouraged his daughter to work on reconfiguring the disparate parcels of land into a unified whole with the help of landscape architect Warren H. Manning of Boston.[9] Manning, an accomplished landscape architect who had worked in the office of Frederick Law Olmsted before going out on his own, had previously created landscape designs for Mr. Pope's friend J. H. Whittemore, and for Whittemore's son, Harris. Pope asked Whittemore for a letter of introduction to Manning and then wrote to Theodate in 1898, "Yes, I should say go ahead with road making, wall building and tree planting this autumn, taking the advice of Mr. Manning in so doing."[10] Historians have questioned Manning's impact on the project. Documents such as Pope's letter, however, urging Theodate to consult Manning, along with the fact that the two met on three different occasions between 1896 and 1898 and that Manning submitted a nominal invoice for a "plan expense" in 1898—an invoice the Popes paid—all suggest some participation on the landscape architect's part.[11]

Each of Manning's visits predated the construction of the house, and, in some cases, the purchase of the land on which the house was eventually built. Thus, it is likely that Manning advised on property selection, as well as specific planning issues such as the siting of the house, the placement of gardens, and the location of the entry drive. There is evidence in Theodate's correspondence, however, that the budding designer may not have responded favorably to Manning's involvement on her project. While working on another architectural commission several years later, Theodate complained to her father that she did not especially like Manning and that she would be willing to see him only if he did not "butt in" on her plans.[12]

Hill-Stead does, however, exhibit numerous characteristics associated with Manning's landscape principles, including a strong sensitivity to natural site features, which gave the estate an unusually close fit to the land. Typical of Manning's work was the incorporation of existing features such as orchards and stone walls; the use of multiple vistas across the land to structure the composition; and the careful siting of the house on a rise, which afforded the best views of the distant landscape at the same time it ensured good drainage and beneficial breezes.[13] The house and farm buildings stood at approximately the same elevation.[14] The multiple panoramic views from the house across the valley encompass the farm buildings, the farmland, the surrounding hills, and the ridges beyond to form an idyllic rural landscape.

Although much of the Farmington River Valley was fertile, the land chosen by the Popes was not the richest in the area. A retreating glacier had strewn rocks and boulders across the terrain. One of the first challenges the Popes faced was converting these rocky fields into productive farmland. Workers cleared the fields and constructed stone walls with the rock, establishing a sense of order to the land. The terrain was gradually manipulated and sculpted to drain the fields, provide tees and greens for the golf course, and form a three-quarter-acre pond nestled in a valley between the hills. The pond, created by damming a brook, became one of the most multifaceted and useful features on the property: it served as a water hazard for the golf course, supplied ice for the estate, and increased the perceived depth and height of the terrain. The resulting two views north, from the house, and south across the pond and back toward the house, were highly picturesque.

A narrow road a little more than half a mile long winds its way through the estate linking the house and barns, estate entrance, and service entrance. Shaded by an allée of sugar maples, the main approach to the house was functional, informal, and inviting. Auxiliary roads wound through the property in a serpentine branching of farm trails, sheep runs, and paths.

Adjacent to the house, Theodate established a sheltered refuge in the tradition of a colonial New England farmstead. With an architect's eye, she directed workers to dig elm trees from the fields and woodlots, and transplant them to create a grove that would screen the house. Digging the mature trees by hand proved an arduous task, as did hauling them by horse and cart to the area around the west facade. But once established, the grove of thirty-odd elms created a domestic atmosphere and an intimate human scale that contrasted well with the vastness of the view across the valley to the hills beyond.

Although the period did not favor foundation planting, Theodate placed about a dozen small, cone-shaped shrubs in a loose row across the front facade. From this point the meticulously maintained lawn sloped gently away from the house. In an interview, a gardener at Hill-Stead recounts the steps taken to care for the lawn at Hill-Stead:

> *Mrs. [Theodate Pope] Riddle objected to mechanized lawn mowers, and insisted that*
> *all the lawns be cut by hand mowers, and that the grass be kept shaggy, or around 2"*
> *high, which was her idea of a proper British lawn. She would become upset, if on one*
> *of her walks about the lawns she found a dandelion, plantain or buttercup. We hand-*

LETTER TO CLASSMATE AGNES HAMILTON

SEPTEMBER 26, 1898 (AGE 31)

Now you may be surprised to hear that father has purchased 150 acres immediately surrounding my land here and is to build in the spring. Isn't that pretty fine for me? It seems too good to be true. Now I want to know if your Aunt Margaret would sell father two or three trees on her estate here for moving? We want some nice large trees and are going to attempt moving some and we hoped she would feel like letting us get a very few of hers very soon.

TOP: Rock-filled field under cultivation at Hill-Stead. Photographed by the Pope's farm manager, Allen B. Cook, ca. 1902. Cook marked the photograph "Sampling of Plowing at Hill-Stead." MIDDLE: The house and carriage barn as seen from the farm complex, ca. 1902

Mature elm trees were moved during the late fall and early winter months after they had shed their leaves, ca. 1900.

weeded on our knees the main lawn several times a season. It always looked exceptional,
or like a photograph of a British lawn in Country Life.[15]

In contrast with the extended views across the landscape, two ornamental
gardens provided more intimate outdoor rooms near the house. The Sunken Garden
was situated slightly off-axis from the south entrance to the house and in view from
the Dining Room and Master Bedroom. This was Ada Pope's garden, created at
the inception of the estate. Probably designed by Theodate with direction from her
mother, it bore all the hallmarks of the Colonial Revival style: low walls, simple
boxwood-lined geometric beds, utilitarian features, and a plant palette of foxgloves,
hollyhocks, phlox, roses, and lilies. Proud of the garden, Theodate and her mother
often entertained friends and family there.

Eight- to ten-foot-high stone walls defined the garden, sited within an
asymmetrical depression in the ground. The walls served to accentuate the garden's
lowered position. The garden measured about 120 feet by 120 feet and was bordered
by an oblong hedge of hemlock. Together, the walls and hedges filtered views of the
landscape beyond, creating a feeling of containment and seclusion within. Theodate
placed an octagonal 25-foot-long summerhouse along the garden's main axis, just

The elm trees provided a shaded refuge on the front lawn at Hill-Stead in the tradition of a colonial New
England farmstead, 1902.

View into Sunken Garden
from Dining Room

LETTER TO HER PARENTS

JUNE 30, 1907 (AGE 40)

I had an hour and a half in the summer house yesterday toward evening—all alone and I thought I must take up some tapestry work in order to reproduce a very beautiful view in the garden. Start with the red of the green house chimney, the grey roof and stone walls, the blue curtain in window, the green in the trees, and come down straight from the chimney, making a long picture, to the garden walk with flowers at either side.

View into Sunken
Garden from Master
Bedroom

beyond the midpoint of the space. Its position created the illusion of a longer path and larger garden. Geometric perennial and annual flowerbeds separated by turf paths extended from the summerhouse in three directions. Dwarf conifers added structure and vertical accents. A boxwood-lined brick walk traversed the garden, passing through the summerhouse and terminating at a sundial designed by Theodate.

A well-worn copy of *The Book of Sun-Dials* rests on a shelf in the Library at Hill-Stead. Theodate copied generously from this treatise, originally compiled in 1900 by Mrs. Alfred Gatty, the leading authority on the subject. Theodate's design of the sundial can be traced back to this book, as can the mottos she had inscribed on it. One motto, originally composed by the Reverend Greville J. Chester and carved on the sundial's base, corresponds with the compass points:

North: Amyddst ye fflowres, I tell ye houres.
East: Soe man shall ryse, Above ye skyes.
South: Beyond ye tombe, ffreshe fflowrets bloome.
West: Tyme wanes awaye , As fflowres decaye.[16]

Summer House and Sunken Garden looking west from pergola, *American Homes and Gardens*, February 1910

Under the shade of the summerhouse Ada Brooks Pope (center) entertains friends. Wood and brick pergola covered with grapevines in background. Seen over the stone wall, the top of greenhouse runs the length of the image, ca. 1902. Photograph by Theodate Pope.

Ada Brooks Pope enjoying the view of her newly planted Sunken Garden, ca. 1902.

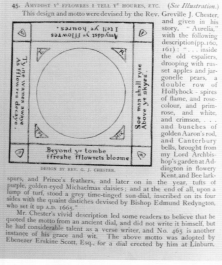

LEFT: Poem inscribed on the sundial's base as diagrammed in *The Book of Sun-Dials*, 1900

RIGHT: The sundial looking north toward summerhouse

The geometry of the Sunken Garden and Summer House is made evident in this aerial view.

On the upper face of the sundial's pedestal, an inscription penned by the Reverend S. E. Bartleet reads, "My noiseless shadow cries, In speech heard by the wise, Against delay."[17] Theodate also had carved along the edge of the top stone a Latin phrase attributed to Hippocrates that was much quoted by Art and Crafts devotees: "Ars Longa Vita Brevis" (art is long, life is short).[18]

A second brick path lined the inner circumference of the Sunken Garden, repeating the octagonal design. A large, horseshoe-shaped grass panel separated the hemlock hedge from the stone walls. In the southeastern corner, along a raised terrace and adjacent to a wall, stood a brick and wood pergola covered with grapevines. An article in the September 1901 *Farmington Magazine* mentions the garden overflowing with boxwood, foxgloves, hollyhocks, phlox, and lilies.[19] Nine years later, a review in the February 1910 issue of *American Homes and Garden* describes it as sumptuous:

> *All around are beds of old fashioned flowers, growing with*
> *the brilliant luxuriance of plants that spare nothing in their*
> *bloom, and which are planted in great masses. It is a charming*
> *place, and one of great simplicity. In one corner of the outer*
> *enclosure is a short flight of stone steps beneath a pergola covered*
> *with grape vines. Above, and without, is the conservatory, the*
> *path beside it being dahlia-bordered on the right and left,*
> *splendid lines of the most brilliant colors, blooming with*
> *quite audacious loveliness, and offering, apparently, an endless*
> *variety of shapes and colors.*[20]

A sampling of invoices stored in the archives of the Hill-Stead Museum, dated 1913, indicates that Ada planted her garden with a bright, contrasting color palette, using strong reds, oranges, blues, and yellows, and underplanted with silver-leaved foliage. She placed bright red *Rosa* 'My Maryland' next to the reddish orange *Rosa* 'Sunburst.' She sowed vivid blue *Anchusa italica* and purple *Eupatorium* next to brilliant yellow *Helenium* and the deep golden coneflowers of *Rudbeckia maxima*. Deep clear-blue *Lobelia*, red blazing star (*Liatris squarrosa grandiflora*), the tall red *Phlox decussata* 'P. Fordham,' and several colors of scented Sweet William completed the spectacle. The soft colors of pink *Dianthus plumarius* and silver-leaved *Artemesia lactifolia*, and the fluffy blooms of white baby's breath (*Gypsophila*) accented the dazzling plantings. She

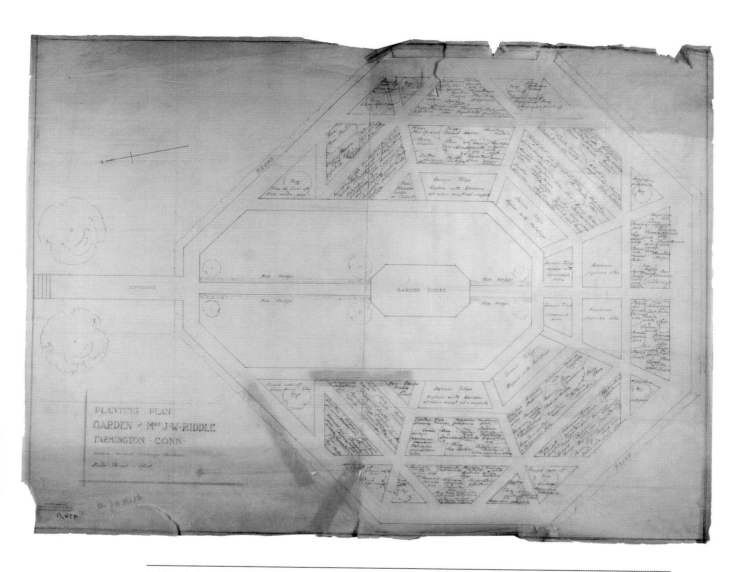

Undated planting plan for the garden of Mrs. J. W. Riddle (Theodate Pope Riddle), Beatrix Farrand, ca. 1920.

TOP: Walking, or Wild, Garden path and rush-seat benches. Less structured than the Sunken Garden, this informal garden provided the visitor with a quiet, shaded space for repose.

BOTTOM: This upper-level path in the Walking Garden hugs the garden's stone wall enclosure and is edged with fieldstones. Here the second-tier path is made of fieldstone. A wood and brick pergola can be seen in the background, along with a few sheep grazing in the adjacent pasture.

was especially fond of single and double varieties of hollyhocks and installed one bed filled entirely with dahlias.

This first garden was replaced by a second. Around the time of her mother's death in 1920, Theodate's friend and colleague, the noted landscape architect Beatrix Farrand, redesigned the Sunken Garden.[21] Farrand drew a garden plan for it that called for the removal or replacement of most of Ada's plants.[22] The flowers that the two women agreed upon exhibited softer pastel shades similar to the colors featured in Alfred Pope's Impressionist art collection, rather than Ada's reds, oranges, and yellows.

The drawing suggests plantings that remained low to the ground at the front of the beds along the walkways and then crescendoed into tall masses along the rear of the beds flanking the hedges. It includes a spring planting plan of Darwin tulips in the six beds along the brick path, followed by summer annuals, including verbena, heliotrope, and lavender, which would have filled the air with gentle fragrances while visitors lingered along the pathways or rested in the summerhouse. Although there is no evidence in the Hill-Stead Museum records confirming the execution of Farrand's design, Theodate and Farrand showed enormous respect for each other's abilities.[23]

The Sunken Garden fell into decline during World War II, and for many years it was nothing more than a patch of mown grass. Farrand's involvement came to light in the 1980s, during a project to revitalize the garden, and the museum's director made the decision to replant following the Farrand design. Changes made to the original plan allowed for easier access by museum visitors and included wider brick paths and a stand of clipped yew. The museum staff and volunteer garden committee made substitutions for period plants (varieties of the original species, for the most part) where the variety was no longer available or suitable to the growing conditions. Today the plantings continue to be updated and interpreted using the Farrand plan. Selections of heirloom plants most like those available to Farrand in the 1920s are added to the garden on a regular basis.

Another now-overgrown garden adjacent to the Sunken Garden is accessible through a break in the right axis of the hedge. This, the Walking, or Wild, Garden, perhaps reflects the influence of the Irish-born designer William Robinson (1838–1935).[24] Robinson's books were widely read at the turn of the twentieth century, and many estate owners adopted his concept of the wild woodland garden as a landscape ideal. Created around the same time as Ada Pope's original Sunken Garden, this Walking Garden similarly offered the visitor a quiet, intimate space for repose

Yew hedge enclosure of the Sunken Garden ringed by stone wall. Sheep pasture accessible through garden gate.

Stone wall–lined approach to Hill-Stead along the main entry drive

and contemplation. The plantings in the Walking Garden were less structured or constrained within their boundaries, however, giving it a relaxed, informal character. Although some of the same plants could be found in both gardens, the plants in the Walking Garden—including hemerocallis, artemisia, ferns, vinca, phlox, *Liatris*, hosta, iris, and *Eupatorium*—were generally hardier and required less maintenance than those used in the Sunken Garden.

Photographs of the Walking Garden probably taken sometime between 1900 and 1910 show an arched stone bridge and stone paths meandering past lush shrubs, perennials, unmown turf, and rush-seated benches. The main entry drive and a stone wall ran along the western edge of the entire garden. The gradual rolling of the terrain allowed for a portion of the garden to be two-tiered. There, the stone path branched in two: the upper-level path had a wide, pebbled surface and was lined with large boulders; running parallel, the lower-level path consisted of stepping stones set into lush grass. A small pond provided extra delight. A mix of evergreen and deciduous trees, including spruce, white pine, maple, oak, and elm, offered contrasting areas of dense shade and dappled sunlight.

The Hill-Stead landscape contained other notable features. A kitchen garden once lay on the east side of the house, tucked discreetly behind a white picket fence and partially enclosed by a stone wall. Here the Popes raised vegetables as well as roses for display in the house. Apples and peaches grew in two separate orchards located on the estate.

Stone walls dominate the Hill-Stead landscape. Some of them existed before the estate was constructed, and the Popes built others. In addition to the walls enclosing the Sunken Garden, three- to four-foot-tall walls lined both sides of the main entry drive. These enhanced the sense of arrival while separating the road from the pasture to the west. Other stone walls formed similar boundaries throughout

TOP LEFT: On Alfred Pope's six-hole golf course the first shot of the day overlooks the pond. Hill-Stead carriage barn and house visible on the opposite hill. Photograph by Theodate Pope. TOP RIGHT: Hill-Stead's herd of about twenty-five prize-winning Guernsey cows were of the finest stock procurable, leading one local reporter in 1907 to describe the "bossies" as being cared for in a manner that would make some human beings envious. The Hill-Stead farm also had a large flock of Dorset and Southdown sheep, pigs, and a team of carriage horses and workhorses. BOTTOM RIGHT: The farm and gardens at Hill-Stead required many working hands, ca. 1902. BOTTOM LEFT: The estate's water system was carefully designed to serve both the house and farm. This pump house borders the pond in the center of the property and directed the water supply to the farm complex.

the complex, defining the farm fields and setting them off from the more formal ornamental gardens and lawns near the house. A stone wall protected the Sunken Garden from the sheep pasture to the south. Another wall ran along the west lawn adjacent to the house and terminated at the kitchen garden, demarcating the edge of the domestic zone.

Hill-Stead had two greenhouses. Typical features of country estates of the period, sadly they are no longer standing. With the assistance of a head gardener and three under gardeners, the Popes grew grapes and peaches in these enclosures. They also started seedlings and propagated flowers. The greenhouses boasted colorful displays of chrysanthemums, azaleas, cyclamen, hibiscus, bougainvilleas, gesneriads, orchids, and oleanders, and they teemed with the heady scents of freesias and camellias.

An avid sports fan, Alfred Pope saw to it that a tennis court and a golf course (or "golf grounds" as he called them) formed part of Hill-Stead's attractions. He had the grass tennis court constructed to the west of the Sunken Garden along the entry drive between 1900 and 1901. It was aligned north to south in order to avoid playing into the rising or setting sun. The six-hole golf course had begun to take shape by November 1900, when Theodate recorded in her diary, "[T]he Baileys came Friday. Had a busy day showing them over the house—having the golf grounds staked out...."[25] The course was in use by July 1901, at which time Theodate wrote, "Harris Whittemore and Father went over the golf course for the first time Saturday after tea, Mother, Justine following."[26] Both men enjoyed a competitive round of golf and could now play on each other's property: J. H. Whittemore had built a course on his Middlebury, Connecticut, farm a few years earlier.[27]

The layout of the six-hole course, which occupied most of the hillside along the road leading to the farm complex, made use of the rolling hills and pasture land, and incorporated the pond and occasional trees as obstacles. Pope particularly enjoyed practicing his game by trying to see how many balls he could hit over the pond, as Theodate noted in her diary on September 30, 1901:

> At supper we got into a gale of laughter over father and the golf links. We were
> wondering what the gardeners think of him. They harrow & roll & cut & weed the
> links & weed & cut & roll & harrow. Father goes out on them every day alone &
> drives a few balls into the pond. And these are the same Italians who dug the pond.
> What do they think of a man who would dig a pond and then fill it up with balls.[28]

Although Theodate prided herself on the quiet and unassuming life the family lived at Hill-Stead, an estate of its size and importance relied on many people to make it run smoothly and efficiently. In 1902, the Popes employed approximately twenty-three full- or part-time employees. In addition to the many farmhands, there were also gardeners dedicated solely to the care of the ornamental gardens and greenhouses.

Following the death of her father in 1913 and of her mother in 1920, Theodate assumed sole possession of Hill-Stead. During the difficult post–World War I period and throughout the Great Depression, her beloved country estate remained a working farm. During World War II, fuel rationing caused a scaling back of farm operations to a fraction of their prewar levels. It was during this time that the high-maintenance Sunken Garden was removed and planted over with turf. The golf course reverted to pasture. The Walking Garden gradually deteriorated.

The most dramatic change to the landscape occurred with the loss of the elm trees around the house. Only three remain on the entire property today, the rest having succumbed to Dutch elm disease beginning in the late 1940s. Their loss changed the once-intimate scale of the house's surroundings and diminished the dramatic contrast of close and distant views across the valley. The orchards, too, suffered serious losses. A killing frost in 1918 effectively wiped out Hill-Stead's peach orchard, along with Connecticut's entire peach industry. And whereas in 1920 there were approximately two hundred apple trees on the property, today less than a dozen remain. Researchers have yet to determine what killed them off.

Throughout her lifetime Theodate steadfastly worked to preserve her childhood dream of a simple life, lived on a rural New England farm. Hill-Stead provided an apt setting for her preferred lifestyle: a lifestyle she shared with other affluent people at the turn of the twentieth century. The landscape she assembled and crafted into Hill-Stead combined aesthetic considerations, leisure activities, and agricultural experimentation. This hybrid landscape, formed out of vernacular traditions, personal interests, and diverse cultural inspirations, remains today a vital manifestation of a revived colonial farmstead.

HARTFORD COURANT, AUGUST 8, 1907

THE UNION MEETING OF THE CONNECTICUT POMOLOGICAL SOCIETY AND THE CONNECTICUT STATE DAIRYMEN'S ASSOCIATION, HELD YESTERDAY ON THE A. A. POPE ESTATE, HILL-STEAD FARM, FARMINGTON, BY INVITATION OF MISS THEODATE POPE, WAS A THOROUGH SUCCESS. IT WAS ESTIMATED THAT ABOUT 400 MEMBERS OF THE TWO ASSOCIATIONS WERE PRESENT FROM ALL OVER THE STATE, AND THEY ARRIVED IN DETACHMENTS BY TRAIN AND TROLLEY DURING THE MORNING HOURS. MOST OF THE VISITORS REACHED THE FARM BEFORE 11 O'CLOCK, AND SPENT THE TIME THAT INTERVENED BETWEEN THEN AND LUNCH IN LOOKING OVER THE MAGNIFICENT ESTATE WITH ITS MANY MODERN IMPROVEMENTS.

A MORE DESIRABLE PLACE FOR A MEETING OF THE ASSOCIATIONS THAN THE HILL-STEAD FARM COULD NOT BE IMAGINED AND THE TIME PASSED QUICKLY FOR THOSE PRESENT. THE FARM COMPRISES ABOUT 300 ACRES, MOST OF WHICH LIES ON THE MOUNTAINSIDE, JUST EAST OF FARMINGTON VILLAGE, AND SUPPORTS, BESIDES A DOZEN HORSES AND THIRTY SHEEP, ABOUT TWENTY-FIVE REGISTERED GUERNSEY CATTLE OF THE FINEST STOCK PROCURABLE, WHICH ARE CARED FOR IN A MANNER THAT WOULD MAKE SOME HUMAN BEINGS ENVIOUS. THE "BOSSIES" ARE CAREFULLY GROOMED DAILY, ARE NOT SUBJECTED TO ANY UNNECESSARY NOISE, DRINK WATER FROM A STERILIZED TROUGH, AND ARE APPROACHED ONLY BY WHITE-SUITED EMPLOYEES WHO TREAT THEM WITH ALL THE DEFERENCE DUE THE ARISTOCRACY OF COWDOM.

LEFT: Hill-Stead's many farm buildings, including sheep shed, horse and hay barns, toolshed, icehouse, drive shed, shepherd's cottage and farmhouse from northeast, ca. 1900 BELOW: Attendees of the Union meeting on lawn in front of house

The stone walls of Hill-Stead do more than frame the landscape. They support it physically, anchor it chronologically, and lend it a unique character. Most importantly, they channel the visitor's experience, both on to and off of the site.

Without the physical support of the low and generally obscure stone walls along old carriage roads, the woodland trails of Hill-Stead would be washed away as gullies or submerged by marsh and swamp. There would be no Sunken Garden. The retaining walls that surround it are strong, tall, and earthy. They create a theater-sized topographic basin with a comfortable sense of enclosure: a hard, straight edge for the soft center of the garden itself.

Without the chronology provided by the stone walls, Hill-Stead would not be so fully grounded in time. The expansive views to the north and west take in a patchwork of old farmstead walls. Most probably date from the Yankee period, though some likely originated in colonial times. These somewhat ragtag walls impart classical stonework traditions and a sense of human antiquity to the site.

Views to the east and south take in the volcanic Metacomet Ridge, which appears to guard Hill-Stead like a rock shelter. Indeed, one of the parcels of farmland amassed to create the 250-acre estate was named "Underledge." This is geologically apt. During the Jurassic period, between 145 to 200 million years ago, this place was a semiarid rift basin, whose rivers and lakes would swell with monsoon rains and on whose shores dinosaurs would roam. The geological result was the sunbaked, reddish brown sandstone that now decorates walls throughout the property.

The artistry of Hill-Stead's walls is created in part by placing naturally jagged, polygonal-shaped rock next to stones smoothed by glacial rough handling. Gray stones predominate but red rocks are inserted randomly for effect. Lichen and mosses provide additional color and texture.

On several occasions in the Jurassic period, lava gushed forth from great fissures, spread out over the basin, and hardened into a greenish black rock called basalt (locally known as traprock). Because the layer of basalt was much more resistant to erosion than was the sandstone, today it forms the spine of the tall ridge overlooking Hill-Stead from the southeast. Much later, between about 17,000 and 30,000 years ago, this ridge was scoured by an invading ice sheet, which broke up the basalt into countless stones. Additional stones were created by active frost processes that took place during the several millennia after the ice retreated, but before the forest returned.

Under Theodate's Pope's watchful eye, workers gathered volcanic stones whose surface was tarnished to a dull gray patina washed by a tinge of green and whose naturally jagged polygonal shapes were only slightly smoothed by glacial rough handling. Instead of avoiding the rounder, reddish brown sandstone boulders, she had workers randomly insert them among the darker, duller volcanic blocks. A third type of stone was also incorporated in the walls: far-traveled exotics, carried in by the glacier from older highlands to the north. Within this group are banded brown gneiss, bronze mica-rich schist, pink pegmatite granite, and cotton-ball quartz.

Theodate had her walls bridge the gap between the simpler style of farmstead walls and the more formal style typical of architectural masonry. Although they look like drystone walls, most are not: below a top tier of loose stones lies a carefully hidden bead of mortar that keeps the top intact. And although her walls look like country stone "fences," many stand higher on one face than the other, meaning that they actually function as retaining walls. Though the stones look like they were "stacked" one above the other, many were laid consciously to avoid separating the stones into the horizontal courses and tiers so typical of brickwork and estate walls, respectively. By preventing a horizontal grain, she could enhance the mosaic pattern called for by the polygon-shaped stones.

The walls flanking the main drive at Hill-Stead serve not only as elegantly constructed retaining walls but also as important design features on the property. Like the experience of ultimately crossing Hill-Stead's threshold, the sensation of passing through the ornate and intentionally narrow main entry gate at Mountain Road signals the visitor's transportation to a special place. This sensation grows as one travels up the undulating slope to the house. It seems that Theodate went out of her way to center the road between walls that are taller and configured more regularly

The opening of the stone wall marks the original pedestrian access from the village of Farmington to Hill-Stead's greensward and front entrance.

than is structurally necessary. Working in concert with the sweeping curve of the road, the walls prevent the visitor from seeing the house right away. This "blinder" effect increases the sense of leaving one world and entering another. It is an effect perhaps inspired by the set of colonial-era walls that bordered the lane leading from Theodate's first permanent home in Farmington, the O'Rourkery, to the future site of Hill-Stead, between which the architect often walked as a young woman.

I've often tried to imagine Hill-Stead without its stone walls. I simply cannot.

Mrs. John Wallace Riddle

Hill-Stead
Farmington
Connecticut

Mrs. John Wallace Riddle

Hill-Stead
Farmington
Connecticut

HILL-STEAD
P.O. FARMINGTON CONNECTICUT
TELEPHONE FARMINGTON 456
RAILROAD STATION HARTFORD
- TELEGRAMS VIA HARTFORD -

HILL-STEAD
FARMINGTON
CONNECTICUT

Stationery displayed on
Theodate Pope Riddle's
secretary in the Master
Bedroom

INTRODUCTION

1   Henry James, *The American Scene* (New York: Harper & Bros., 1907), 46.

2   John La Farge and August F. Jaccaci, *Concerning Noteworthy Paintings in American Private Collections* (New York: August F. Jaccaci Co., 1909), 257–258.

3   Mark A. Hewitt, *The Architect and the American Country House* (New Haven, Conn.: Yale University Press, 1990), 157, 163.

4   Barr Ferree, "Notable American Homes: 'Hill-Stead,' the Estate of Alfred Atmore Pope, Esq., Farmington, Conn.," *American Homes and Gardens* vol. 7 (Feb. 1910): 47.

5   Ibid., 45.

6   Theodate Pope Riddle. Last Will and Testament (April 1946), 15, Archives, Hill-Stead, Farmington, Connecticut.

7   See Marilee Boyd Meyer, *Inspiring Reform: Boston's Arts and Crafts Movement* (Wellesley, Mass.: Davis Museum and Cultural Center, Wellesley College, 1997).

HILL-STEAD AND ITS ARCHITECT

1   Julius Gay, *Farmington, Connecticut: The Village of Beautiful Homes* (Farmington, Conn.: Arthur L. Brandegee and Eddy H. Smith, 1906), 7.

2   Barr Ferree, "Notable American Homes: 'Hill-Stead,' the Estate of Alfred Atmore Pope, Esq., Farmington, Conn.," *American Homes and Gardens* vol. 7 (Feb. 1910): 45.

3   This essay draws principally on the following scholarship: Sharon Dunlap Smith, *Theodate Pope Riddle: Her Life and Architecture*, (http://www.vali-net.com/~smithash/); Sandra L. Katz, *Dearest of Geniuses: The Life of Theodate Pope Riddle* (Windsor, Conn.: Tide-Mark, 2003); Julia Sienkewicz, "Hill-Stead" report prepared for the Historic American Building Survey (HABS) in 2006; and Mark A. Hewitt, "The Making of an American Country House," *The Magazine Antiques* (Oct. 1988): 849–60; as well as Hill-Stead itself, its Archives, and its staff.

4   For more on New England vernacular building traditions, see Thomas C. Hubka, *Big House, Little House, Back House, Barn* (Hanover, N.H.: University Press of New England), 1984.

5   Introduction, in Richard Guy Wilson, ed., *Re-Creating the American Past: Essays on the Colonial Revival* (Charlottesville: University of Virginia Press, 2006), 5.

6   Julia Sienkewicz, "Hill-Stead" (Historic American Building Survey Report, 2006). Prepared for the Historic American Building Survey (HABS), 106. Report and related images available online at the Library of Congress's "American Memory" website at memory.loc.gov. Search for Hill-Stead's report under the heading architecture, landscape.

7   Richard Guy Wilson, *The Colonial Revival House* (New York: Harry N. Abrams, Inc., 2004).

8   Theodate Pope, Diary, 13 Feb 1889, Archives, Hill-Stead, Farmington, Connecticut.

9   Ibid., 9 Dec 1900. Folios (or "Parts") I through IV bear copyright dates of 1898 to 1899; V–VIII, 1900–1901; IX–XII, 1902, so Theodate was likely to have had only the first group of plates and, perhaps, some of the earlier ones in the second group.

10   Joy Wheeler Dow, *American Renaissance* (New York: William T. Comstock, 1904), 18.

11   Ibid.

12   Theodate Pope, Diary, 14 Sept. 1900, Archives, Hill-Stead Museum.

13   See James F. O'Gorman, *Connecticut Valley Vernacular: The Vanishing Landscape and Architecture of the New England Tobacco Fields* (Philadelphia: University of Pennsylvania Press, 2002), 28–48.

14   See Sarah Allaback, *The First American Women Architects* (Urbana-Champaign: University of Illinois Press, 2008).

15   Theodate Pope, Diary, 24 May 1889, Archives, Hill-Stead Museum.

16   Elizabeth G. Grossman and Lisa B. Reitzes, "Caught in the Crossfire: Women and Architectural Education, 1880–1910," in *Architecture: A Place for Women*, ed. Ellen Perry Berkeley (Washington and London: Smithsonian Institution Press, 1989), 27–40, esp. 37 n. 9. There is in the Archives at Hill-Stead a small collection of student architectural and engineering drawings (studies of machine parts, perspective construction, sciagraphy, and the like) that have been attributed to Pope. See Smith, *Theodate Pope Riddle*, chap. 1. The drawings are unsigned, however, and there is no external evidence to support this attribution.

17   Katz, *Dearest of Geniuses*, 157. Avon Old Farms was built by Theodate Pope Riddle between 1918 and 1929. Her plans for the school were never fully realized in her lifetime. The school continues to operate, and much of its continued growth is guided by Theodate's original designs.

18   Sienkewicz, 49–50; Smith, *Theodate Pope Riddle*, chap. IV (reproducing only a portion of the sheet). At the New-York Historical Society there are redrafts of these elevations by L. D. Ayres of the McKim, Mead & White office dated 30 November 1898. (Copies of these redrafts are also held in the Archives at Hill-Stead.)

19   Ibid., 48.

20   Leland Roth, *McKim, Mead and White, Architects* (New York: Harper & Row, 1983), 24.

21   Cited in Hewitt, "The Making of a Colonial Country House," 854.

22   *Farmington, Connecticut: The Village of Beautiful Homes* (Farmington, Conn.: Arthur L. Brandegee and Eddy H. Smith, 1906), 185–186.

23   J. H. Whittemore to Theodate Pope, 4 Dec. 1895, copy, Archives, Hill-Stead, #W-1556.1.

24   See James S. Ackerman, *The Villa: Form and Ideology of Country Houses* (Princeton, N.J.: Princeton University Press, 1990).

25   Katz states source as: Theodate Pope Diary, 1886, Hill-Stead. However, nothing to the effect of Theodate's dislike of the Cleveland house can be found in the 1886 diary.

26   Theodate Pope to the firm of McKim, Mead & White (collection, New York Historical Society). The letter is reproduced verbatim in Smith, *Theodate Pope Riddle*, appendix A, Archives, Hill-Stead, copy, #978.

27   Archives, Hill-Stead, copy, #539.

28   Theodate Pope to William Rutherford Mead, Walter Cain Collection, Avery Architectural Library, Columbia University, New York. The letter is reproduced verbatim in Smith, *Theodate Pope Riddle*, appendix B; #2193, Archives, Hill-Stead.

29   Ibid.

30   McKim, Mead & White Papers, Folder M-13, Pope House, 29 September 1898 (New-York Historical Society).

31   Theodate Pope to McKim, Mead & White, undated, #978, Archives, Hill-Stead.

32   Alfred Atmore Pope to Theodate Pope, 29 Sept. 1898, #546, Archives, Hill-Stead.

33   Sienkewicz, 106.

34   Theodate Pope to Egerton Swartwout, 26 and 31 October 1898, #979 and #983, respectively, the McKim office, Archives, Hill-Stead Museum. Both letters make reference to the perspective drawing. In an undated note #982, surely to Swartwout, she wrote, "Before drawing the important perspective of house for father and mother please be sure of all details so that general effect will be right. But if you do it yourself as I hope you will, you will know just what I wish." (McKim, Mead & White Papers, New-York Historical Society.)

35 Theodate Pope, Diary, 14–19 March 1901, Archives, Hill-Stead. Her diary notes being in Virginia, but does not mention going to Mount Vernon. However, a photo of her at Mount Vernon indicates that the time her diary entry was written coincided with her trip to the site.

36 Thedodate Pope, Diary, 29 Oct. 1901, Archives, Hill-Stead.

37 This porch is usually described as Grecian in style, but detailing—here and throughout Hill-Stead—is based on Roman, not Greek, precedent. It was originally conceived as flat roofed and topped with Chippendale railings similar to the Mount Vernon–style portico and the bay windows of the west elevation. The revised plan altering the north wing dated 18 October 1906 and signed by C. N. Elliot is inscribed "Cols. and details similar to old office Porch." See also the section through the service wing of 20 April 1899 with later, light pencil sketch of a preliminary design. McKim, Mead & White Papers, New-York Historical Society.

38 The 1899 plan also shows what would have been unsightly prominent bulkheads leading into the basement at the base of the Kitchen and Laundry walls.

39 I quote from the Dover reprint (1965) of the English translation by Isaac Ware, *The Four Books of Andrea Palladio's Architecture* (London, 1738), 38. The author derives his principle from the disposition of the human body.

40 *The Georgian Period*, vol. II, part VI, plate 24.

41 Barr Ferree, "Notable American Homes: 'Hill-Stead,' the Estate of Alfred Atmore Pope, Esq., Farmington, Conn.," *American Homes and Gardens* vol. 7 (Feb 1910): 46–47.

42 Ibid., 47.

43 Ibid., 45.

44 Ibid., 45.

45 Theodate Pope, Diary, 14 Sept. 1900, Archives, Hill-Stead.

46 Theodate Pope, Diary, 3 Dec. 1900, Archives, Hill-Stead.

47 Ibid.

48 For a complete list of buildings see Smith, *Theodate Pope Riddle*, "Catalogue of Buildings," 117–130.

49 Katz, *Dearest of Geniuses*, 75. Gilbert may have judged Westover from photographs exhibited at the Architectural League of New York in 1910. Harold Roth, FAIA, of New Haven, in numerous conversations with the author in the course of their long friendship.

50 Katz, *Dearest of Geniuses*, 189.

51 In 1922 Theodate Pope (then Riddle) was awarded the Leoni W. Robinson Prize of the Architectural Club of New Haven. Robinson (1852–1923) had trained with the pioneering Connecticut architect Henry Austin (1804–91), so that award linked Pope historically to the earliest years of the profession in the state. In 1940 she received the diploma and silver medal from the Fifth Pan-American Congress of Architects held at Montevideo, Uruguay. *National Cyclopaedia of American Biography* (New York: James T. White & Company, 1943), vol. 30.

FURNISHINGS

1 I wish to acknowledge the generous assistance of Cindy Cormier and Melanie Bourbeau in the preparation of this essay. They shared their deep knowledge of the house, photocopied many items of interest, and allowed me to spend hours looking at the furnishings of the house. Time within the rooms of Hill-Stead proved invaluable.

Henry James, *The American Scene* (1907; repr. New York: Penguin, 1994), 37.

2 The key documentary source for the Euclid Avenue home interior is a 1913 photo album given by Harris Whittemore to Ada Pope, currently in the Hill-Stead Archives, Farmington, Conn. For more on Emerson, see Cynthia Zaitzevsky, *The Architecture of William Ralph Emerson, 1833–1917* (Cambridge, Mass.: Fogg Museum of Art, 1969). For an interpretation of these images, see Clarence Cook, *The House Beautiful: Essays on Beds and Tables, Stools and Candlesticks* (1881; repr. New York: Dover, 1995).

3 The range of Morris & Co. products displayed at the exhibition was published in the firm's catalog

The Morris Exhibition at the Foreign Fair: Boston, 1883–84 (Boston: Roberts Brothers, 1883).

4   Cook, *The House Beautiful*, 121–23, 146–51. Cook's remarks were echoed by others, including the architect Claude Bragdon (1866–1946), who complained about the Victorian "age of rubbish," when commercially available things "usurp[ed] space in this crowded modern world" and women were terrorized by the "tyranny of inanimate objects." See Bragdon's "The Architecture of the Home," *House Beautiful* 16, no. 1 (June 1904): 10, 48. Like Cook, Bragdon called for the simplicity of antiques and art as an antidote to the overwhelming quantity of commercial furnishings.

5   Cook, *The House Beautiful*, 121.

6   For more, see Alice Cooney Frelinghuysen, "Patronage and the Artistic Interior," in *Herter Brothers: Furniture and Interiors for a Gilded Age*, ed. Katherine Howe, et al. (New York: Harry N. Abrams, 1994), 78–104; and Kathleen Pyne, "Portrait of a Collector as an Agnostic: Charles Lang Freer and Connoisseurship," *The Art Bulletin* 78, no. 1 (March 1996): 76. For a theoretical discussion of the motives of these industrialists, see Pierre Bourdieu, *Distinction: A Social Critique of the Judgement of Taste* (Cambridge, Mass.: Harvard University Press, 1984).

7   Theodate Pope Riddle to Mr. F. Swenston, undated [written just after Ada's death in 1920], letter 1021, Archives, Hill-Stead Museum, Farmington, Conn. On A. H. Davenport, see Anne Farnham, "A. H. Davenport and Company, Boston Furniture Makers," *Antiques* 109, no. 5 (May 1976): 1048–55; and Farnham, "H. H. Richardson and A. H. Davenport: Architecture and Furniture as Big Business in America's Gilded Age," in *Tools and Technologies: America's Wooden Age*, ed. Paul Kebabian and William Lipke (Burlington, Vt.: Robert Hull Fleming Museum, 1979), 80–92.

8   On the early history of the O'Roukery, see Julia Sienkewicz, "Hill-Stead," Historic American Buildings Survey Report, 24–27. Report and related images available online at the Library of Congress's "American Memory" website at memory.loc.gov. Search for Hill-Stead's report under the heading architecture, landscape.

9   Theodate Pope Riddle, Memoirs, 1937, #4113–32, copy in Archives, Hill-Stead Museum.

10   Cook, *The House Beautiful*, 187–90. Like Cook, designer (interiors and textiles) Candace Wheeler also called for the use of antiques in an aesthetic manner, in her *Principles of Home Decoration* (New York: Doubleday, Page & Co., 1903). On Wheeler's brand of Colonial furnishing, see Jean Dunbar, "Candace Wheeler and the New Old-Fashioned Home," in *Recreating the American Past: Essays on the Colonial Revival*, ed. Richard Guy Wilson, et al. (Charlottesville, Va.: University of Virginia Press, 2006), 40–52.

11   Sienkewicz, "Hill-Stead," 26–27. Several books in the Popes' library are inscribed by George Dudley Seymour or have his bookplate pasted in them.

On Hartford as an important early center in antique collecting, see Elizabeth Stillinger, *The Antiquers* (New York: Knopf, 1980); and William Hosley Jr., "Hartford's Role in the Origins of Antiques Collecting in America," in *New England Collectors and Collections*, ed. Peter Benes (Boston: Dublin Seminar for New England Folklife, 2006), 102-116.

It is striking that the spare historical decorating scheme of Theodate's O'Rourkery closely resembles the historic house museums and interior photographs of Wallace Nutting, which would become popular during the first decade of the twentieth century. For more on Nutting, see Thomas Denenberg, *Wallace Nutting and the Invention of Old America* (New Haven, Conn.: Yale University Press, 2003).

12   Theodate Pope Riddle to Mr. F. Swenston, undated, letter 1021.

13   See John Harris, *Moving Rooms: The Trade in Architectural Salvage* (New Haven, Conn.: Yale University Press, 2007), esp. 101–49; and Nicholas Penny and Karen Serres, "Duveen and the Decorators," *The Burlington Magazine* 149, no. 1251 (June 2007): 400–6.

14   Miscellaneous receipts and Theodate Pope's diary, 1888–89, Archives, Hill-Stead Museum.

15   Ada Pope to Theodate Pope, September 1898, #542, Archives, Hill-Stead; and Sienkewicz, "Hill-Stead," 64–72.

16   A. H. Davenport to McKim, Mead & White, October 29, 1900, Department of Prints, Photographs, and Architectural Collections,

Collection PR042, box no. 366, folder no. Pope AA, New-York Historical Society. Stanford White had given Ada permission to have such a copy made. The breakfront was originally placed in the Library but was subsequently moved to the Dining Room, where it is currently located. Melanie Bourbeau kindly shared the contents of the Davenport letter, a copy of which is held in the Hill-Stead Museum Archives.

17 Alfred Pope to J. H. Whittemore, April 27, 1900, and #W620, assorted receipts, Archives, Hill-Stead Museum.

18 The distinctive approach of the Popes is made clear by comparison with the 1888 house of J. H. Whittemore, which was designed by McKim, Mead, & White and built in Naugatuck, Conn. Though the Whittemores were close friends of the Popes—often traveling together to Europe and purchasing many of the same types of art and decorative furnishings, such as mezzotints of English artists, Japanese woodblock prints, and sang-de-boeuf and celadon ceramics—the interiors of the Whittemore home were more in line with the New York aesthetics of elaborately detailed interior architecture, aesthetic movement wallpapers and textiles, and dense furnishings. Ann Smith kindly shared her research on the Whittemore family with me in an e-mail of 23 March 2008.

19 This attribution is based on the existence of remnants of the hall carpet with "Whittall" woven on the back in the Archives of the Hill-Stead Museum. For information on Whittall, I am grateful for the research undertaken at the Worcester Historical Museum by Katie Rogers, a curatorial intern at Hill-Stead during the summer of 2000 (her notes are held in the Archives).

Matthew J. Whittall was born in Kidderminster, England, in 1843, and trained in the carpet business in Stourport there. He emmigrated to Worcester, Massachusetts, by 1870, when he was the first superintendent of the Crompton Carpet Company. In 1879 he imported looms from England and established his own, very successful carpet company that expanded multiple times between 1884 and 1910 to an operation with about fifteen hundred employees. Charles Washburn, *Industrial Worcester* (Worcester, Mass.: Davis Press, 1917), 100–4.

In 1908, Alfred Pope bought seventy-eight yards of English Wilton carpet and ninety-one yards of Axminster carpet from the Boston importer Torrey, Bright & Capen for the Euclid Avenue house; and in 1911 Ada Pope bought thirty and a half yards of Saxony Brussels from the same Boston firm for her brother Edward Brooks of Andover, Mass. #2069 (receipt of purchase, Feb. 9, 1911), Archives, Hill-Stead Museum.

20 In the Hill-Stead Archives are rolls of paper with the same pattern, but in a different color, that were used in the hall outside the pantry on the first floor. Marked by M. H. Birge & Sons, they are the basis for this attribution. On the switch from British reform papers of the 1870s and 1880s to the revival styles that began to become popular at the turn of the century, see Catherine Lynn, *Wallpaper in America from the Seventeenth Century to World War I* (New York: W. W. Norton, 1980), 367–478. The same exact paper was used by Wallace Nutting in the renovation of the Wentworth-Gardner House, in Portsmouth, New Hampshire, in 1915–16. Denenberg, *Wallace Nutting*, 3.

21 Theodate's attentiveness to color, in particular, is evident in the diary she kept during the family's European trip from the end of 1888 through the summer of 1889. There she comments on the colors used in Rubens's paintings hanging in the Church of St. Jacques, Antwerp. She also praises the yellow silk hangings in one room in the Escorial Palace in Spain, as well as the way in which each room was appointed with hangings of a distinctive color. Theodate Pope, diary, 1888–1889, Archives, Hill-Stead Museum.

On William H. Jackson & Co., see Sienkewicz, "Hill-Stead," 61, 65. This well-known New York firm has offered a wide assortment of historically styled fireplace equipment and mantels since 1827.

22 The 1909 inventory describes the chandelier as an "old colonial bronze chandelier fitted with eight astral lamps…taken from Old Salem House." This description may be a reference to a Brooks family house in Salem, Ohio, or to another Salem, such as Salem, Massachusetts. Theodate was known to have visited the latter in 1886 to look at the early American homes there. With the exception of this chandelier, the gas wall sconces and other chandeliers placed throughout the house were ordered from Shreve, Crump & Low in Boston. The columnar lamp on the center table had bas-relief panels of Hercules made by Pierre-Philippe Thomire of Paris.

23 The photographs show a card table in each niche flanking the fireplace, but the 1909 inventory suggests that French marquetry commodes replaced these tables. These commodes also featured swag decoration.

24 The ceiling height in the Ell Sitting Room is 8'6", a full foot less than in the Drawing and Dining Rooms.

25 The photographs of the Dining Room seem to have been taken shortly after the Popes moved into Hill-Stead. *The Architectural Record*, 1902, illustration of the room, along with *The Architectcural Record*, 1906, and *American Homes and Gardens*, 1910, published images contain the same suite of Empire chairs and china cupboard. These had been replaced by the time the 1909 inventory was conducted, at which time the shield back chairs and Empire sofa table currently in the Dining Room and the china cupboard currently in the Second Library were located in the Dining Room. Oak had associations more with the seventeenth-century; most eighteenth-century paneling was pine that was painted.

26 On the Davenport dining table, see Sienkewicz, "Hill-Stead," 67. Several of the shield back chairs have new backs and replaced arms. The reworked nature of the furniture is also evident in the knife boxes, which are devoid of their interior partitions and used as decorative urns.

27 Today, only *Jockeys* still hangs in the Dining Room, so it has been necessary to recreate the original scheme by juxtaposing the images, the inventory, and the room's architecture

28 The cabinet, marked "Duveene" in the 1909 inventory, and the ceramics it housed are now located in the Second Library. By 1909, the breakfront secretary bookcase shown in the older photographs was moved out to the room-sized south porch, which featured multipaned windows that could be removed to create an open-air porch.

29 While only the desk is listed in the inventory, the Russian bronze samovar converted to a lamp sat upon either a table or a chest in the 1902 and 1906 photographs.

30 The 1910 photograph illustrates a different bureau than that listed in the 1909 inventory but otherwise offers an accurate view of the items listed in the inventory.

31 On Freer and the concept of "agnostic aesthetes," see Kathleen Pyne, "Portrait of a Collector," 75–97.

32 On the Gilded Age interiors, see Arnold Lewis, *The Opulent Interiors of the Gilded Age* (original edition New York: D. Appelton, 1883-84; reprinted New York, Dover, 1987). On the contemporary taste for French eighteenth-century interiors, see Edith Wharton and Ogden Codman Jr., *The Decoration of Houses* (1897; repr. New York: W. W. Norton, 1997).

33 Bragdon, "The Architecture of the Home.," 10.

34 See Elsie de Wolfe, *The House in Good Taste* (1913; repr. New York: Rizzoli, 2004). Although a few of de Wolfe's ideas seem to pertain to the Popes' work, her interest in a broader historical period that included the seventeenth century and her reliance on painted furniture, simple painted walls, and chintz distinguish her.

35 For a good summary of this interest in a purer form of American style, see Nancy McClelland, *Furnishing the Colonial and Federal House* (Philadelphia: J. B. Lippincott Company, 1936). For a recent assessment of McClelland's influence, see Bridget May, "Nancy Vincent McClelland (1877–1959): Professionalizing Interior Decoration in the Early Twentieth Century," *Journal of Design History* 21, no. 1 (March 2008): 59–74. Wallpaper in Hill-Stead's Dining Room was made in France for Nancy McClelland.

36 Nancy Curtis and Richard Nylander, *Beauport: The Sleeper-McCann House* (Boston: David Godine, 1990).

37 On James, see Thomas Otten, "*The Spoils of Poynton and the Properties of Touch*," *American Literature* 71, no. 2 (June 1999): 263–90.

THE PAINTINGS

1 Henry James, *The American Scene* [travel essays written in 1904–05, published as a book in 1907] (New York: Horizon Press, 1967), 46.

2 Glasgow University Library, Glasglow, Scotland. A copy of this letter, #958, is held in the Archives, Hill-Stead Museum, Farmington, Connecticut. Alfred Atmore Pope to James McNeill Whistler, 22 September 1894.

3 Camille Pissarro, *Letters to His Son Lucien*, ed. John Rewald (New York: Pantheon, 1943), 248.

"Nabob" refers to a viceroy or deputy governor under the former Mogul empire in India. More generally, it is a person of wealth and prominence.

4   Alfred Atmore Pope to Harris Whittemore, 25 August, 1894. Harris Whittemore Jr., Trust, Naugatuck, Conn. A copy of this letter, #W778, is held in the Archives, Hill-Stead Museum.

5   Ibid.

6   Ibid.

7   Alfred Atmore Pope to J. H. Whittemore, 7 November 1888. Harris Whittemore Jr., Trust, Naugatuck, Conn. A copy, #W266, is held in the Archives, Hill-Stead Museum.

8   Alfred Atmore Pope to Harris Whittemore, 26 August 1894, copy, #W779, Archives, Hill-Stead Museum.

9   See Judith Barter, ed., *Mary Cassatt, Modern Woman* (Chicago: The Chicago Art Institute, 1998).

10   See Anne Distel, *Les Collectionneurs des impressionnistes: Amateurs et marchands* (Düdingen/Guin: Editions Trio, 1989), especially chapter XXI, "Les Havemeyer [sic] et les premiers collectionneurs amércains."

11   Roger Fry, *Characteristics of French Art* (London: Chatto and Windus, 1932), 122; Roger Fry, *Cézanne: A Study of His Development* (Chicago: University of Chicago Press, 1927), 24.

12   In addition to those at Hill-Stead, another excellent example of properly framed Impressionist paintings is the collection of the Brooklyn Museum, re-done by curator Elizabeth Easton based on her extensive research into the history of mid- and late-nineteenth-century frames.

13   Theodate Pope, Diary, 28 March 1886, Archives, Hill-Stead Museum.

14   Ibid., 11 June 1887.

15   Ibid., 23 August 1889.

16   Frances Weitzenhoffer, *The Havemeyers: Impressionism Comes to America* (New York: Harry N. Abrams, 1986), 146–47. For selected correspondence between Mary Cassatt and Theodate Pope, see Nancy Moull Matthews, ed., *Cassatt and Her Circle: Selected Letters* (New York: Abbeville Press, 1984).

17   Ibid.

18   Theodate Pope to William Rutherford Mead, 17 September 1898, Avery Library, Columbia University, New York. A copy of the letter, #2193, is held in the Archives, Hill-Stead Museum.

19   *The Architectural Review* 9, no. 11 (November 1902): 282–83.

20   See the essay "Hill-Stead and Its Architect," by James F. O'Gorman in this volume.

21   Barr Ferree, "'Hill-Stead,' the Estate of Alfred Atmore Pope, Esq., Farmington, Conn.," *American Homes and Gardens* 7, no. 2 (February 1910): 45.

22   Kenyon Cox, in John La Farge and August F. Jaccaci, *Concerning Noteworthy Paintings in American Private Collections* (New York: August F. Jaccaci Co., 1909), 257-258. "Haden" refers to Francis Seymour Haden (1818-1910). He was an English surgeon, etcher, collector, and writer. He was influenced by James McNeill Whistler, his brother-in-law, to take up etching and was active in the etching revival of the late nineteenth century.

23   Weitzenhoffer, *The Havemeyers*, 146–47.

24   *Testament of Nélie Jacquemart*, 19 January 1912. Two versions in Musée Jacquemart-André archives, Paris, France, dated the same day. All quotes are from version "A."

25   Last Will and Testament of Theodate Pope Riddle, memorandum, page 5, 10 January 1946, Archives, Hill-Stead Museum.

THE LANDSCAPE, GARDENS, AND FARM

1   These farms were influenced by the Romantic Movement of the mid-eighteenth century. The intention was to create a country estate laid out as a pastoral paradise, with barns and animals for farming, and a designed landscape with picturesque walks and pleasing views.

2   "Farmers Have Field Day in Farmington," *The Hartford Courant*, 8 Aug 1907.

3   Everett E. Edwards, *A Bibliography of the History of Agriculture in the United States* (New York: Burt Franklin, 1970).

4   Theodate Pope, Diary, 8 March 1887, Archives, Hill-Stead, Farmington, Conn. Late in her life, Theodate fostered three children who lived at Hill-Stead.

5   Edwin Morris Betts, *Thomas Jefferson's Garden Book, 1766–1824, with Relevant Extracts from His Other Writings* (Charlottesville, Va.: Thomas Jefferson Memorial Foundation, 1944).

6 For additional information on the Arts and Crafts movement and the history of gardening in America, see Judith B. Tankard, *Gardens of the Arts and Crafts Movement: Reality and Imagination* (New York: Harry N. Abrams, 2004); and Walter T. Punch, ed., *Keeping Eden: A History of Gardening in America* (Boston: Little, Brown & Company, 1992).

7 For additional information on English parks and gardens, see Edward Hyams, *The English Garden* (New York: Harry N. Abrams, 1966).

8 Compiled from *The Valley Herald & Journal*, 27 August 1898, Registry of Deeds notations, a historic map dated Aug./Sept. 1898, Archives, Hill-Stead Museum.

9 For a detailed overview of Manning's long and productive career, see Lance Neckar, "Developing Landscape Architecture for the Twentieth Century: The Career of Warren H. Manning," *Landscape Journal* 8 (Fall 1989): 78–91.

10 Alfred Atmore Pope to Theodate Pope, 11 Sept. 1898, #540, Archives, Hill-Stead Museum.

11 Warren H. Manning, journal daybook, 1897–1903, no. 53, Warren H. Manning Collection, Book No. 53, Center for Lowell History, University of Massachusetts, Lowell. No plans, sketches, or design notes from his hand are known.

12 "Mr. Whittemore is going to have Mr. Manning come out next Tuesday—you know the landscape architect. Mr. Whittemore said he wanted his advice about the Catholic church. He was very nice saying he knew I did not like Manning. I told him that made no difference at all—would be glad to see him unless he tried to butt in about the locating of school." Theodate Pope to Alfred and Ada Pope, June 1907, #738-3/3, Archives, Hill-Stead Museum. The subject of the letter is Westover School, Middlebury, Conn.

13 For Manning's principles of landscape design, see Warren Henry Manning, *Stout Manual Training School Handbook for Planning and Planting Small Home Grounds* (Menomonie, Wis.: Stout Manual Training School, 1899), 1–13.

14 The house site is approximately 335 feet above sea level; the farm complex is approximately 300 feet above sea level.

15 Myron Erickson, interviewed by John Crockett (no date), Archives, Hill-Stead. .

16 Mrs. Alfred Gatty, *The Book of Sun-Dials*, ed. by H. K. F. Eden and Eleanor Lloyd (London: George Bell and Sons, 1900), 210.

17 Ibid., 343.

18 Ibid., 213. Perhaps in Theodate's enthusiasm to transcribe the romantic verses on each side of her sundial, she failed to consider the final scale of the piece. She had specified that it should be 40 inches square and 47 1/2 inches high, including plinth and pedestal. Shortly after its placement in the garden, she told her diary, "The sundial is up and I am worried over it. It seems too large." Despite such misgivings it remains in place, unmoved and unchanged."

19 G. L., "In the Farmington Gardens," *Farmington Magazine*, vol. 1, Sept. 1901:1.

20 Barr Ferree, "'Hill-Stead,' The Estate of Alfred Atmore Pope, Esq., Farmington, Connecticut," *American Homes and Garden*, vol. 7, Feb 1910: 51.

21 It is not known exactly when Theodate Pope and Beatrix Farrand first met. In 1912, Farrand was commissioned to design a garden at Westover School in Middlebury, Connecticut. As architect of the school, Theodate was more than likely consulted on this decision and it was perhaps at this time that the two women met. In 1919, the two submitted a joint proposal for the design of a Women's Reform School for the state of Connecticut. While they did not win the competition, they again came together on a design project.

22 The original, undated graphite-on-trace planting plan (plan no. 976, Residence of Mrs. J. W. Riddle, Farmington, Conn.) is stored in the Beatrix Farrand Collection at the Environmental Design Archives, University of California, Berkeley. A copy of the Farrand plan exists in the Hill-Stead Museum Archives. For more on Farrand's life and works, see Jane Brown, *Beatrix: The Gardening Life of Beatrix Jones Farrand, 1872–1959* (New York: Viking, 1995); and Diana Balmori, Diane Kostial Mcguire, and Eleanor M. McPeck, *Beatrix Farrand's American Landscapes, Her Gardens and Campuses* (New York: Sagapress, 1985).

23 Farrand's plan is now preserved at the University of California, Berkeley.

24 William Robinson, *The English Flower Garden* (1883; reprinted New York: Amaryllis Press,

1984); William Robinson, *The Wild Garden* (1895; reprinted Portland, Ore.: Sagapress/Timber Press, 1994).

25 25 November 1900, Archives, Hill-Stead Museum.

26 Theodate Pope, Diary, 17 July 1901, Archives, Hill-Stead Museum. Justine was Harris Whittemore's wife.

27 In 1881 there were fewer than a dozen golf courses in the United States. The first public course in New England appeared in 1891. It was quickly followed in 1892 by the region's first private course, on the property of Arthur Hunnewell in Wellesley, Massachusetts. Maintaining one's own private course became one of the pleasures of wealthy industrialists and other prominent men of the era: Vanderbilt, Rockefeller, Havemeyer, DuPont, Whittemore, and St. Gaudens families all owned courses. See Herbert Warren Wind, *The Story of American Golf* (New York: Farrar, Straus and Company, 1948).

28 Theodate Pope, Diary, 30 September 1901, Archives, Hill-Stead Museum.

Allaback, Sarah. *The First American Women Architects.* Urbana-Champaign: University of Illinois Press, 2008.

Brown, Jane. *Beatrix: The Gardening Life of Beatrix Jones Farrand, 1872–1959.* New York: Viking, 1995.

Denenberg, Thomas Andrew. *Wallace Nutting and the Invention of Old America.* New Haven, Conn.: Yale University Press, 2003.

Dow, Joy Wheeler. *American Renaissance.* New York: William T. Comstock, 1904.

Farmington, Connecticut: The Village of Beautiful Homes. Farmington, Conn.: A. L. Brandegee and E. H. Smith, 1906.

Ferree, Barr. "'Hill-Stead,' The Estate of Alfred Atmore Pope, Esq., Farmington, Connecticut." *American Homes and Gardens* 7 (February 1910): 45–51.

The Georgian Period: A Collection of Papers Dealing with "Colonial" or XVIII-Century Architecture in the United States. Edited by William Rotch Ware. 17 folio vol. Boston: American Architecture Company, 1899–1902.

Glenn, Thomas Allen. *Some Colonial Mansions and Those Who Lived in Them: With Genealogies of the Various Families Mentioned.* 2 vols. Philadelphia: Henry T. Coates & Company, 1899–1900.

Hayward, Allyson M. "Hill-Stead Museum: Historic Landscape Report." Watertown, Mass.: Reed Hilderbrand Associates, 2002.

Hewitt, Mark A. "The Making of an American Country House." *The Magazine Antiques* (October 1988): 849–60.

"House of Alfred A. Pope, Farmington, Connecticut." *The Architectural Review* 9 (1902): 282–83.

Katz, Sandra L. *Dearest of Geniuses: The Life of Theodate Pope Riddle.* Windsor, Conn.: Tide-mark Press, 2003.

Manning, Warren H. "The Garden and Lawn: Laying Out Home Grounds." *The Canadian Horticulturist* 16 (1893): 280–83.

Manning, Warren H. *A Handbook for Planning and Planting Small Home Grounds.* Menomonie, Wis.: Stout Manual Training School, 1899.

"Mr. Alfred A. Pope's House." *The Architectural Record* 20 (August 1906): 122–29.

Neckar, Lance. "Developing Landscape Architecture for the Twentieth Century: The Career of Warren H. Manning." *Landscape Journal* 8 (Fall 1989): 78–91.

Otten, Thomas. "The *Spoils of Poynton* and the Properties of Touch." *American Literature* 71, no. 2 (June 1999): 263–90.

Re-Creating the American Past: Essays on the Colonial Revival. Edited by Richard Guy Wilson, Shaun Eyring, and Kenny Marotta. Charlottesville: University of Virginia Press, 2006.

Robinson, William. *The Wild Garden.* New York: Scribner and Welford, 1881.

Sienkewicz, Julia. "Hill-Stead." Historic American Buildings Survey Report. 2006.

Smith, Sharon Dunlap. "Theodate Pope Riddle: Her Life in Architecture." http://www.valinet.com/~smithash

Tankard, Judith B. *Beatrix Farrand: Private Gardens, Public Landscapes.* New York: Monacelli Press, 2009.

Thorson, Robert M. "Final Report on the Stone Walls of Hill-Stead Museum, Farmington, Connecticut: Inventory, Measurement, Interpretation, and Recommendations." Unpublished Manuscript, Hill-Stead Archives, Farmington, Conn. 2006.

Wheeler, Candace. *Principles of Home Decoration.* New York: Doubleday, Page & Company, 1903.

Wilson, Richard Guy. *The Colonial Revival House.* New York: Harry N. Abrams, 2004.

EDITOR AND ESSAYIST

James F. O'Gorman is Grace Slack McNeil Professor Emeritus of the History of American Art at Wellesley College and writes, lectures, and consults on the history of architecture. Among his many publications are two on Connecticut subjects: *Connecticut Valley Vernacular: The Vanishing Landscape and Architecture of the New England Tobacco Fields* (2002) and *Henry Austin: In Every Variety of Architectural Style* (2009). He has also written on architects Frank Furness, Henry Hobson Richardson, Louis Sullivan, and Frank Lloyd Wright.

ESSAYISTS

Edward S. Cooke, Jr., is Charles F. Montgomery Professor of American Decorative Arts at Yale University. Among his many publications are *Upholstery in America and Europe from the Seventeenth Century to World War I* (1987) and *Making Furniture in Pre-Industrial America: The Social Economy of Newtown and Woodbury, Connecticut* (1996). On more recent forms of craft, he has written or contributed to several catalogues, including *Inspiring Reform: Boston's Arts and Crafts Movement* (1997); *Wood Turning in North America Since* 1930 (2001); and *The Maker's Hand: American Studio Furniture, 1940–1990* (2003). Cooke's museum experience was in the American Decorative Arts and Sculpture department at the Museum of Fine Arts, Boston. He received his Ph. D. in American and New England Studies from Boston University.

Allyson M. Hayward is a landscape historian, lecturer, and author of *Norah Lindsay: The Life and Art of a Garden Designer* (2007). She is a graduate of the Landscape Institute of Harvard University and for several years served as chair of the New England Garden History Society. In 2003 she was awarded a Gold Medal by the Massachusetts Horticulture Society for her work promoting New England's garden history.

Anne Higonnet received her Ph. D. from Yale University in art history, and is currently professor of the history of art at Barnard College of Columbia University. Among her publications are *Pictures of Innocence: The History and Crisis of Ideal Childhood* (1998); *Berthe Morisot's Images of Women* (1992); and *Berthe Morisot, A Biography* (1990/1995). Her current book project, *Collectors and Their Museums: From the Wallace Collection to Dumbarton Oaks,* is in production.

Robert M. Thorson is professor of geology at the University of Connecticut, where he holds a joint appointment between the Department of Ecology and Evolutionary Biology and the Department of Anthropology. His most recent books on stone walls are *Exploring Stone Walls: A Field Guide to New England's Stone Walls* (2005) and *Stone By Stone: The Magnificent History in New England's Stone Walls* (2002). Currently in press is his book entitled *Beyond Walden: The Hidden History of America's Kettle Lakes and Ponds* (2009). He also coordinates the Stone Wall Initiative within the Connecticut State Museum of Natural History and writes a regular op-ed column for *The Hartford Courant.*

Robert A. M. Stern, F.A.I.A., is Dean of the School of Architecture at Yale University and founder and senior partner of Robert A. M. Stern Architects of New York City. His professional work is the subject of many publications, and he is the author of many more. In 1986 he wrote *Pride of Place: Building the American Dream* (1986), which accompanied a popular television series on American architecture, including the work of Theodate Pope.

Melanie Anderson Bourbeau is Associate Curator of Hill-Stead Museum. She received her master's degree in American studies from Trinity College, Hartford, Connecticut, and has worked at numerous museums in Greater Hartford including The Mark Twain House and Museum; The Noah Webster House in West Hartford, Connecticut; and the Austin House, a house museum operated by the Wadsworth Atheneum Museum of Art in Hartford.

Cynthia A. Cormier is Director of Education and Curatorial Services at Hill-Stead Museum. She received her master's degree in art history from the University of Massachusetts in Amherst. Before coming to Hill-Stead in 1998, she held the position of Curator of Education at the Wadsworth Atheneum Museum of Art in Hartford and Curator at Wistariahurst Museum in Holyoke, Massachusetts. She chairs the editorial board of *Connecticut Explored,* a magazine of Connecticut history.

PHOTOGRAPHERS

Lesley Unruh is an editorial, fine art, and commercial photographer. She holds a BFA in Photography and Graphic Design from the Savannah College of Art and Design. Prior to pursuing her freelance career, Lesley served as a Photographer and Photo Producer for Condé Nast. Lesley's work has appeared in numerous interior and art publications. She lives in Brooklyn, New York.

Jerry L. Thompson has been working as a professional photographer since 1973. He studied at the University of Texas and at Yale with Walker Evans. He has held Guggenheim and NEA fellowships and has been photographer-in-residence in the American Wing of the Metropolitan Museum of Art. His photography may be found in the permanent collection of various major American museums. He has also written several books on photography.

ARCHIVAL SOURCES

Ashfield Historical Society, Howes Brothers Collection, Ashfield, Mass.155, 169 (bottom right)

Environmental Design Archives, University of California, Berkeley, Calif.163

Hill-Stead Museum, Farmington, Conn.

Diaries and Letters: 26, 35–7, 41, 51–2, 63, 65, 71, 77–8, 87, 101, 125, 131–2, 153, 157

Photographs and Drawings: 11, 22, 27–8, 30, 32–4, 39, 61–2, 69–70, 74, 81, 85, 103, 109, 114, 120, 138 (left), 149 (top), 154, 160, 169 (top left, top right, bottom left), 173

Manuscript pages: 48, 49 (left), 161 (top left)

Board of Governors Collection: 93

New-York Historical Society, McKim, Mead & White Collection, New York City, N.Y. 45, 56–8, 66, 72

Wellesley College Library, Wellesley, Mass. 49 (right)

IMAGE CREDITS

ARCHIVAL PHOTOGRAPHS

Ashfield Historical Society, Ashfield, Mass.

Howe's Brothers Collection 155, 169 (bottom right)

Hill-Stead Museum Archives, Farmington, Conn.

Allen B. Cook: 149 (top), 154, 169 (top right, bottom left), 173 (top)

American Home & Gardens: 42, 76, 95 (bottom), 99 (top), 104, 159

The Architectural Record: 21, 90, 95, 138 (right)

The Architectural Review: 93 (top)

George M. Edmundson: 22, 85

Gertrude Käsebier: 11, 32, 74 (left), 86, 160 (bottom)

Karl Klauser: 33 (top), 61

Theodate Pope Riddle: 74 (right), 109 (right), 120 (right), 138 (left), 160 (top), 169 (top left)

Unknown: 27, 28, 30, 33 (bottom), 34, 39, 70, 81, 103, 114, 120 (left), 173 (bottom)

CONTEMPORARY PHOTOGRAPHS

James Rosenthal: 161 (top right), 177

Patty Swanson   : 9, 99 (bottom), 167

Jerry L. Thompson: 6, 12, 16, 76 (bottom), 82, 91, 118, 137, 140, 146, 149 (bottom), 161 (bottom), 166

Leslie Unruh: cover, 2, 25, 46, 73, 97, 100, 102, 106–7, 108, 110, 112–13, 126, 130, 133, 134, 145, 156, 158, 174, 178, 188, 190, 193